**Architecture of
Indonesia**

Architectural Guide
Indonesia

From 1945 to the Present

Edited by Imelda Akmal

Contents

Index of Works 9
Introduction 13

A Jabodetabek 28
B Java 142
C Bali 242
D Other Islands 324
E Vernacular 360

Index of Buildings 381
Index of Architects 383
Authors 386
Photo Credits 387

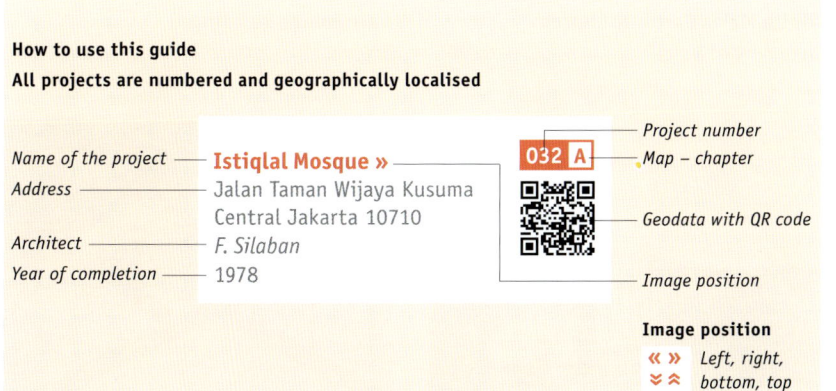

How to use this guide
All projects are numbered and geographically localised

Name of the project —— **Istiqlal Mosque »** —————————— Project number
Address —————————— Jalan Taman Wijaya Kusuma   **032 A** —— Map – chapter
                       Central Jakarta 10710   —— Geodata with QR code
Architect ——————————— F. Silaban
Year of completion ——— 1978   —— Image position

Image position
« » Left, right,
⌄ ⌃ bottom, top

Bina Nusantara International School
Duta Cermat Mandiri .... page 61

Gelora Bung Karno Main Stadium
F. Silaban .... page 74

Anjung Salihara
Studiodasar .... page 86

West One Marketing Office
Studio TonTon .... page 92

Stella Maris Catholic Church
Duta Cermat Mandiri .... page 105

Parliament Building
Soejoedi Wirjoatmodjo .... page 108

Istiqlal Mosque
F. Silaban .... page 109

Kosenda Hotel
Studio TonTon .... page 114

Said Naum Mosque
Adhi Moersid .... page 118

The Hermitage Hotel
KIAT Architects .... page 126

Bogor Raya School
Indra Tata Adilaras..................... page 139

Cikampek Rest Area
d-associates .... page 141

Selasar Sunaryo Art Space
Baskoro Tedjo .... page 176

Bumi Pemuda Rahayu
Arkom .... page 197

Rumah Turi
tim tiga .... page 209

Guest House Banyuwangi
Adi Purnomo .... page 239

Amarterra Villas
Wastu Adi Olahrupa .... page 270

Potato Head Beach Club Restaurant
andramatin .... page 280

Alila Villas Soori
SCDA Architects .... page 297

Bamboe Koening Restaurant
Effan Adhiwira .... page 307

Novotel Palembang
Duta Cermat Mandiri .... page 345

Mahligai Minang Mosque
Urbane Indonesia .... page 351

Dodoha Mosintuwu
Urbane Indonesia .... page 357

Reconstruction of a North Nias House
Society of North Nias .... page 371

Index of Works

A	Jabodetabek - Jakarta Bogor Depok Tangerang Bekasi	p.28
001	**Soekarno Hatta Airport** *Paul Andreu*	
002	**Bina Nusantara University Alam Sutra** *Duta Cermat Mandiri*	
003	**Sekolah Terpadu Pa Hoa** *Adi Purnomo*	
004	**Multimedia Nusantara University** *Duta Cermat Mandiri*	
005	**Bina Nusantara International School** *Duta Cermat Mandiri*	
006	**Bakoel Koffie** *andramatin*	
007	**Talavera Office Park** *Airmas Asri*	
008	**Gedung Yohanes, Church of St. John the Evangelist** *Han Awal & Partners*	
009	**ASEAN Secretariat** *Soejoedi Wiryoatmodjo*	
010	**Graha Niaga** *Wiratman & Associates*	
011	**Sequis Centre** *UK architect*	
012	**Gelora Bung Karno Main Stadium** *F. Silaban*	
013	**Manhattan Hotel** *Duta Cermat Mandiri*	
014	**Bakrie Tower** *H. O. K. Architect, Urbane Indonesia*	
015	**Dia.Lo.Gue Artspace** *andramatin*	
016	**The Papilion** *d-associates*	
017	**Kemang 89** *Tan Tjiang Ay*	
018	**Komunitas Salihara** *Marco Kusumawijaya*	
019	**Salihara Office** *andramatin*	
020	**Anjung Salihara** *Studiodasar*	
021	**Galeri Salihara** *Marco Kusumawijaya*	
022	**Teater Salihara** *Adi Purnomo*	
023	**West One Marketing Office** *Studio TonTon*	
024	**Omah Architecture Library** *RAW*	
025	**Café Batavia** *Unknown Architect*	
026	**Historical Museum of Jakarta** *J. W. Van der Velde, Boy Bhirawa*	
027	**Museum of Bank Indonesia** *Eduard Cuypers, Han Awal & Partners*	
028	**Museum of Bank Mandiri** *J.J.J. de Bruyn, A. P. Smits, C. van de Linde*	
029	**Gedung Arsip Nasional** *Han Awal, Budi Lim*	
030	**Stella Maris Catholic Church** *Duta Cermat Mandiri*	
031	**DPR/MPR Parliament Building** *Soejoedi Wirjoatmodjo*	
032	**Istiqlal Mosque** *F. Silaban*	
033	**Bank Indonesia** *F. Silaban*	
034	**Monumen Nasional** *Soekarno and Soedarsono*	
035	**Kosenda Hotel** *Studio TonTon*	
036	**Wisma Nusantara** *Wiratman Wangsadinata*	
037	**Hotel Indonesia** *Abel Sorensen*	
038	**Masjid Said Naum** *Adhi Moersid*	
039	**Wisma BNI** *Zeidler Partnership Architects*	
040	**UOB Plaza** *Duta Cermat Mandiri*	
041	**Wisma Dharmala** *Paul Rudolph*	
042	**Kampus Semanggi Universitas Atma Jaya** *Han Awal & Partners*	
043	**Bioskop Metropole** *Liauw Goan Sing*	
044	**Tugu Kunstkring Paleis** *P. A. J. Moojen*	

045	**The Hermitage Hotel**	*KIAT Architects and Thomas Elliott*
046	**Morissey Hotel**	*Aboday*
047	**Kementrian Perdagangan Republik Indonesia**	*Duta Cermat Mandiri*
048	**Hall of University of Indonesia**	*Budi Sukada*
049	**Administrative Centre of the University of Indonesia**	*Gunawan Tjahjono and Team*
050	**Central Library of the University of Indonesia**	*Duta Cermat Mandiri*
051	**Plaza Quantum Electro FTUI**	*Han Awal & Partners*
052	**Bogor Raya School**	*Indra Tata Adilaras*
053	**Cikampek Rest Area**	*d-associates*

B Java p.143

054	**Breeze Art and Boutique Hotel**	*Tan Tjiang Ay*
055	**Sensa Hotel**	*Duta Cermat Mandiri*
056	**Nu Ciwalk**	*Duta Cermat Mandiri*
057	**Concordia**	*Ir. Gmeilig Meyling, Tan Tjiang Ay*
058	**Padma Hotel**	*Kerry Hill*
059	**Salman Mosque ITB**	*Achmad Noe'man*
060	**West and East Halls of ITB**	*Henri Maclaine Pont, Bambang Setia Budi and Team*
061	**Rumah#1 LABO.themori**	*LABO*
062	**Selasar Sunaryo Art Space**	*Baskoro Tedjo*
063	**Gupondoro**	*Oky Kusprianto*
064	**Dusun Bambu**	*APTA*
065	**Al Irsyad Mosque**	*Urbane Indonesia*
066	**Outward Bound Indonesia**	*Andry Widyowijatnoko, Djoko Kusumowidagdo*
067	**Amanjiwo Hotel**	*Ed Tuttle*
068	**Oei Hong Djien Museum**	*d-associates*
069	**Via Via Café Yogyakarta**	*Eko Prawoto*
070	**Cemeti Art House**	*Eko Prawoto*
071	**Greenhost Boutique Hotel**	*tim tiga*
072	**Nasirun Gallery**	*Eko Prawoto*
073	**Ngibikan Village Reconstruction**	*Society of Ngibikan Village, Eko Prawoto*
074	**Bumi Pemuda Rahayu**	*Effan Adhiwira, Marco Kusumawijaya, Yuli Kusworo*
075	**Sendangsono Pilgrimage Complex**	*Y. B. Mangunwijaya*
076	**Maria Regina School**	*Adi Purnomo*
077	**Rempah Rumah Karya**	*tim tiga*
078	**Rumah Turi**	*tim tiga*
079	**Bank Indonesia Solo**	*Eduard Cuypers, Han Awal & Partners*
080	**Bank Indonesia Solo (Extension)**	*Han Awal & Partners*
081	**Javaplant**	*andramatin*
082	**Santa Maria Assumpta Church**	*Y. B. Mangunwijaya*
083	**Open Museum of Trowulan Archaeological Site**	*Han Awal & Partners*
084	**Soekarno Memorial Park**	*Baskoro Tedjo*
085	**Hotel Tugu**	*Duta Cermat Mandiri*
086	**Intiland Tower Surabaya**	*Paul Rudolph*
087	**De Soematra**	*Hidayat Endramukti*
088	**1903 Restaurant**	*Hermawan Dasmanto*
089	**Historica Coffee and Pastry**	*Hermawan Dasmanto*
090	**Hotel Majapahit**	*L. Martin Sarkles, C. P. Wolff Schoemaker*
091	**Musholla Kompleks Banyuwangi**	*andramatin*
092	**Blimbingsari Airport Banyuwangi**	*andramatin*
093	**Pendopo Bupati Banyuwangi**	*Adi Purnomo*
094	**Guest House Banyuwangi**	*Adi Purnomo*

C	**Bali**	p.242

095	**Conrad Wedding Chapel** *Studio TonTon*
096	**Amarterra Villas** *Wastu Adi Olahrupa*
097	**The Bale** *Studio TonTon*
098	**Nusa Dua Tourism Project** *Bali Tourism Development Corporation*
099	**Alila Villas Uluwatu** *WOHA*
100	**Potato Head Beach Club Restaurant** *andramatin*
101	**Ize Hotel** *Studio TonTon*
102	**Villa Alopa** *SHL Asia*
103	**Oasis Lagoon Sanur** *Sonny Sutanto Architects*
104	**Sudamala Suites** *E. S. A. International*
105	**Maya Sanur** *Duta Cermat Mandiri*
106	**Tandjung Sari Hotel** *Wija Wawo-Runtu*
107	**Popo Danes** *Popo Danes Architect*
108	**Alila Villas Soori** *SCDA Architects*
109	**Millenium Bridge** *Bamboo Pure*
110	**Green School** *Bamboo Pure*
111	**Fivelements Puri Ahimsa Healing Centre** *Arte Architect and Associates*
112	**Bamboe Koening Restaurant** *Effan Adhiwira*
113	**Gaya Fusion** *Arte Architect and Associates*
114	**Alila Ubud** *Kerry Hill*
115	**Ubud Hanging Gardens** *Popo Danes Architect*
116	**The Maya Ubud Resort and Spa** *Duta Cermat Mandiri*
117	**Villa Bayad** *Popo Danes Architect*
118	**Puri Wulandari** *Arte Architect and Associates*

D	**Other Islands**	p.324

119	**Novotel Palembang** *Duta Cermat Mandiri*
120	**Arumdalu Eco Resort** *RAW*
121	**Cassia Co-op Training Centre** *TYIN Tegnestue Architects*
122	**Surau Baitul Djalil** *Timmy Setiawan*
123	**Mahligai Minang Mosque** *Urbane Indonesia*
124	**Tsunami Commemoration Museum** *Urbane Indonesia*
125	**Dodoha Mosintuwu** *Effan Adhiwira*
126	**Almarik Hotel Restaurant** *Effan Adhiwira*
127	**Menara Phinisi** *akanoma*

E	**Vernacular Architecture in Indonesia**	p.360

128	**Reconstruction of Uma Pangembe of Wainyapu**
	Society of Wainyapu, Yori Antar, Rumah Asuh Foundation
129	**Reconstruction of Uma Pangembe of Ratenggaro**
	Society of Ratenggaro, Yori Antar, Rumah Asuh Foundation
130	**Reconstruction of a North Nias House**
	Society of North Nias, Yori Antar, Rumah Asuh Foundation
131	**Reconstruction of a South Nias House**
	Society of South Nias, Yori Antar, Rumah Asuh Foundation
132	**Reconstruction of Rumah Gadang of Nagari Sumpu**
	Society of Sumpur, Yori Antar, Eko Alvarez Z., Rumah Asuh Foundation
133	**Wae Rebo Reconstruction**
	Society of Wae Rebo, Yori Antar, Rumah Asuh Foundation

Komodo Islands, a group of islands on western Flores in eastern Indonesia: a beautiful part of the archipelago of a country with more than seventeen thousand islands

Indonesia: A Huge Country with Enormous Diversity

Imelda Akmal

Indonesia is an enormous country to summarise in one book – not only because of its size, but also because Indonesia possesses a long history and outstanding diversity. The geographic span of this country is equal to the distance between London to New York. Indonesia covers 5,193,250 km² and consists of more than seventeen thousand islands, more than six hundred languages, and hundreds of faiths (with only six of them recognised by the state). The numbers are truly mind-blowing. This is because Indonesia is an archipelagic state simultaneously linked and separated by dozens of seas and several oceans. In *A History of Modern Indonesia* (U.S.A.: Stanford Univ. Press, 1993), author M.C. Ricklefs describes how Indonesia began circa 1200 with the spread of Islamic faith, after a period of independent kingdoms from Kutai Kartanegara to Mataram. When Indonesia finally fought for its independence from Japanese and Dutch occupation in 1945, its historical roots remained and created ethnic, cultural, language, religious, and, of course, architectural diversity. Therefore, to present a single subject, namely the architecture of Indonesia, we must provide clear criteria.

To that end – after DOM publishers had invited us to compile the *Architectural Guide Indonesia* – we immediately created boundaries that enabled us to proceed to the next stage. Firstly, it was decided that the buildings selected for the guide were to be buildings designed and erected following independence – from 1945 to the present. This decision was made because the name *Indonesia* was officially used and recognised globally at that time.

Furthermore, several parameters were specified as considerations: the chosen architectural works must have historical value, or constitute milestones in the development of architecture in Indonesia (or at least have a positive influence in the field of architecture), or have a progressive design for their time. Since this book is a visitors' guide to architectural projects in Indonesia, the architectural objects presented within had to be accessible to the public (at least by appointment) and not be private buildings.

These set parameters drastically pinpointed the architectural objects selected for this guide – especially since almost all progressive architects in Indonesia mostly design private homes, while government buildings are built based on administrative and not architectural considerations. Commercial buildings are dominated by economic considerations that make them nothing more than boring, gigantic buildings that contribute little to no positive value to the world of architecture.

The next step was to decide how these architectural works would be presented within the book. The entire area of Indonesia is usually divided based on its geographic position: western Indonesia, central Indonesia, and eastern Indonesia. However, for the purpose of compiling this guide, the method of division was very difficult to accomplish because the economic development and the growth of construction in Indonesia are imbalanced to the point of being extremely lopsided. Jakarta, whose total area is merely 0.3 per cent of the total area of Indonesia, controls more than 80 per cent of the country's economy. Economic centralisation and the top-down political system adopted during the New Order regime (which ruled Indonesia for thirty-two years) are some of the causes. Construction, on the other hand, always follows economic prosperity; therefore the development of architecture in Jakarta and its surrounding area (Jabodetabek) grew intensely, followed by Java, Bali, and Sumatra. Other large islands – such as Kalimantan, Sulawesi, and Papua – are almost entirely bereft of architectural development. These areas are dominated by plantations, mining areas, and forests.

In the end, we observed the balance of the selected works, and decided that chapters should be divided using the following pattern: the first chapter consists of the Jabodetabek area (p. 30), followed by Java, Bali, Sumatra, and lastly the *Other Islands*. Vernacular architecture is also discussed – architecture that was not designed by an architect, but still functions perfectly and is still used. This has a certain significance among some Indonesian ethnicities who still adhere to their old traditions today. Vernacular architecture has also attracted global attention and won international awards. A number of communities and architects have taken action to preserve vernacular architecture, and even studied it in order to create a modern Indonesian architecture rooted in the richness of its culture. To this end, we reserve a special chapter dedicated to vernacular architecture, especially examples involving architects who documented it for the purpose of this book. We hope that our effort means that the *Architectural Guide Indonesia* provides a rich insight into the architecture of Indonesia. Happy reading!

Indonesia has the fourth longest beach in the world: Pink Beach on the Komodo Islands is indisputably one of its most beautiful attractions

As a nautical country, the sea is the source of life: a seaweed plantation like this one on Bali Beach is easy to find

Indonesia used to be a strong maritime motherland but has since transformed into a land-based nation following its independence

Prailing, a traditional village in Sumba Island, eastern Indonesia

Urban village in the city of Surabaya

The diversity of Indonesian people bears a close relation to the richness of their culture and architecture

Monuments were part of Soekarno's propaganda to present the strength of Indonesia following its independence and assert Jakarta's identity as a solid modern nation

An Indonesian Architectural Style

A summary from Iwan Sudrajat's thesis A Study of Indonesian Architectural History

Summary by Imelda Akmal
with permission from Iwan Sudrajat

The search for a national identity has been one of the major quests in Indonesia since its independence. Architecture in Indonesia has been one of the key areas in which a political effort to define and develop a more pronounced national identity and character has been exercised. It is only appropriate to say that architectural practice in Indonesia has been closely bound up with the rise of nationalism and the search of a national identity.

On 17 August 1945, two days after the Japanese surrender, Soekarno and Hatta proclaimed Indonesia's independence. This demonstrated to the Dutch that the Indies had gone forever, displaced by the Republic of Indonesia. Nationalist sentiment burst forth throughout the nation, and the widespread acceptance of Soekarno and Hatta as President and Vice-President of the new republic was a sign of a new unity of purpose among nationalist forces.

The institutional basis of architectural discipline in Indonesia took form in the years immediately after independence. A brief historical survey of significant events during this period provides us with a general overview of the early development of architectural education and practice that led to the present architectural condition. It should be noted that architectural subjects in the Indies had previously always been taught as part of the education of civil engineers. It was not until October 1950, when the first architectural school in the Bandung University of Technology was founded, that architecture gained its status as a discrete discipline. The training programme, starting with twenty students and three Dutch lectures, was primarily modelled after the school where the first lecturers graduated – Delft University of Technology in Netherlands. The training was directed towards the acquisition of expertise in building design, with a focus on limited principal parameters such as function, climate, building construction and materials.

F. Dicke took the position of head of the school. He believed that a starting point could not be found in a period of great prosperity in art and architecture many centuries ago. Moreover, a culture with a spiritual background which was totally different from the present could also not be taken as a basis. He emphasised that if Indonesia wanted to occupy a position in the present world and share in international life, it should not situate itself in an isolated position and search for a national architecture with its eyes closed to what was happening in the world. Architects should rather learn from the architecture of the past how, under certain circumstances, an architectural problem can be tackled and solved, seen in the light of spiritual movements of the time. Architects were recommended to critically select new ideas from international architectural events which were suitable to be assimilated. Finally, architects were also to imbue their concepts with their own ideas and inspirations, so as to play their own instrument in a great global orchestra.

Due to the political conflicts over West Irian, in 1955 all Dutch lecturers were recalled to their homeland, except V.R. van Romondt who nursed the ambition to create a new *Indonesian architecture* which had its roots in Indonesian societies. He shared the view of F. Dicke that architectural monuments of the past should not be considered as ideal examples to be reproduced or revived, but rather as a stimulus for contemporary Indonesian architects to attain great achievements in their own modern context. He insisted that a new cultural basis was needed in order to create a new living architecture for the future. According to van Romondt, the main task for contemporary Indonesian architects was to search for the principles of Indonesian architecture which would serve as a new basis for their future creation. A short circuit in the searching process, such as the adoption of a foreign style alien to the people, or reproducing an ancient historical style which was meaningless in the modern context, was undesirable. What he meant by a new *Indonesian architecture* was an architecture based upon traditional principles but developed in a modern way to satisfy the needs of contemporary society – the fullfilment of the ideas of functionalism, rationalism, and the simplicity of a modern design, but deeply inspired by traditional architectural principles.

By 1958 the number of students at the architectural school in Bandung had increased to a total of five hundred. In September 1959, the Indonesian Architects Association (IAI) was established by graduates, and in 1961 the leadership of the architectural school was fully taken over by Indonesians. By the early 1960s, Western literature had begun to penetrate Indonesian architectural education. The work and concept of master builders, such as Walter Gropious, Frank Lloyd Wright and Le Corbusier, became normative references for class discussion and studio work. The political climate at that time had significantly contributed to the widespread acceptance of modern architectural theories and concepts, such as during the *Guided Democracy* period (1957–1964) under President Soekarno. *Modernity* was given a powerful symbolic importance as a vital index of national unity and strength.

Soekarno was able to influence profoundly the character of architectural production during the years in which he held power. His predilections for the modern, the revolutionary and the heroic in architecture had led him to the institution of a huge building programme for the capital, Jakarta, which at that time was already home to three million people. He hoped to tranform its image as a colonial centre into a capital of a free and sovereign state, and to make it the pride of the nation and the »beacon of the New Emerging Forces«. At the commemoration of Jakarta's 435th anniversary in June 1962, he appealed to, »Build up Jakarta as beautifully as possible, build it as spectacularly as possible, so that this city, which has become the centre of the struggle of the Indonesian people, will be an inspiration and beacon to the whole of struggling mankind and to all the emerging forces within the framework of *nation building*.« This got off to a feverish beginning at the end of the 1950s with the tearing down of old buildings, the erection of new ones, the widening of roads, and the construction of new highways. Skycrapers and modern building technologies, such as air conditioning, elevators and escalators, were introduced to the country for the first time, and Jakarta's skylines have been dramatically changed ever since. Examples illustrating this are the Hotel Indonesia; the Sarinah Department Store; the Gelora Bung Karno; the six-lane Jakarta highway by-pass; the clover leaf bridge crossing Jembatan Semanggi; the National Monument and its Merdeka Square; Istiqlal Mosque and the Wisma Nusantra office building; the Ancol Recreation Centre; the parliament buildings, and a number of sculptural monuments.

Soekarno exerted a strong influence on the character of his architectural projects through personal patronage. Each of his projects was the subject of consultation between the architect and himself since he often conceived the original idea and made suggestions for alterations. Each project bore his signature of approval, without which no action could be taken. Since Soekarno's fall in 1965, the New Order government of General Soeharto has channelled foreign investment into Jakarta and carried through intensive modernisation plans in line with its general aim of economic development for Indonesia. Many of the projects left by Soekarno were completed by the Mayor, General Ali Sadikin, including the parliament building in Senayan, Istiqlal Mosque, Ancol Recreation Centre, and several shopping centres which had received Soekarno's imprimatur. Under Ali Sadikin, Jakarta has gradually transformed into a reasonably well-regulated urban system.

Gelora Bung Karno, a stadium with a capacity of more than 100,000 spectators, was funded by the Soviet Union in the Soekarno era

It should be emphasised that under the government of the New Order, Indonesia had been pursuing a domestic policy based on adherence to the Pancasila maxims *Bhineka Tunggal Ika* (Unity in Diversity). This unity was to be found through the past, by paying homage and respect to the memory of ancestors, by cherishing and maintaining cultural traditions, and by identifying and emphasising common trends that run through obvious differences. President Soeharto and the First Lady, Tien Soeharto, played a central role in the extensive programme of popularising nostalgic evocations of rural Indonesia through the use of ethnic architectural themes. They appeared at cornerstone ceremonies and the inaugurations of many important buildings, whose designs are based on a traditional architectural style. The indiscriminate adoption of a traditional style in many cases reflects the cynical side of New Order architectural propanganda which signifies a desire »to reveal essence and continuity, rather than to record existence and change.«

As far as the problem related to a national architectural style and identity is concerned, it is possible to divide Indonesian architects into at least three different factions. The first group of architects holds the view that Indonesian architecture already exists and comprises

various traditional architectural styles from different regions. The second group is sceptical about any possibility of achieving an ideal national architectural style and identity. The third group, representing the majority of architectural academics, consistently follows the path of its *father figure* van Romondt, and holds the view that Indonesian architecture is still in the process of development, and its outcome will depend on their commitment and critical reappraisal of cultural ideals, aesthetic tastes, and technological means that brought building models and forms into being at a particular historical moment. This group is convinced that a deeper understanding of such principles would offer contemporary architects some insight or inspiration in coping with foreign cultural influence in their own context.

Indonesian architects face the challenge of finding a manner in which to articulate the country's new task and at the same time regain access to a rich local tradition. The main obligation will be to formulate an architectural language which is suitable to deal with contemporary realities. There is no getting away from modernism since modernism is a condition, not just a style. A more accommodating and flexible strategy with regard to local tradition must be adopted and a creative transformation of local types for present-day needs must be explored.

Pitch roofs are symbolic of traditional Indonesian architecture

Jabodetabek (Greater Jakarta)

BEKASI

053

A

0 — 25 km

Jabodetabek: The Booming Mega *Village-City*

Imelda Akmal

When someone says that he or she lives in Jakarta, chances are that he or she does not actually live inside the borders of the administrative city of the Special Capital Region of Jakarta, the capital of Indonesia. He or she may actually live in the areas surrounding Jakarta: i.e. Tangerang, Depok, or Bekasi. This is because Jakarta has now expanded and is virtually united with these areas, creating a huge sprawling area which is commonly abbreviated as Jabodetabek (Jakarta-Bogor-Depok-Tangerang-Bekasi). Perhaps in English it would be apt to call this area Greater Jakarta.

According to the urban observer Marco Kusumawijaya in his book *Kota Rumah Kita*, the idea that Jabodetabek should be thoroughly and harmoniously planned began in the era in which Ali Sadikin was Governor of Jakarta (1966–1977), and the idea persists even now. In the 1980s, under President Soeharto's regime, developers were given the right to open and develop large areas to create new satellite cities to support Jakarta. However, the developments of these satellite cities were not accompanied by decent urban planning and adequate infrastructure, particularly public transport.

A former village, Jakarta has now grown into a giant *village-city* and constitutes the political and economic centre of Indonesia

As a result, commuters prefer to use private vehicles to reach their workplaces. Jakarta, as well as its satellite cities, grew aggressively and sporadically. Today Jakarta is not a city supported by satellite cities, but an amalgamation of satellite cities sprawling into a single gigantic city. There are no rigid boundaries (except administrative ones) between Jakarta and the cities that supposedly support it – no green belts, for instance, that should produce oxygen and be the intermediary areas between Jakarta and its supporting cities. Most citizens are even unable to recognise the boundaries between Jakarta and its satellite cities.

Jabodetabek has thus become an invisible megapolitan area. The region, which is currently home to more than 23 million citizens, is the centre of everything: the economy, politics, industry, and so on. It is also the greatest market and dominant consumer in Indonesia. Marco Kusumawijaya declares that even though the population of this area amounts to only 10 per cent of the whole population of Indonesia, its contribution to the gross regional domestic product (GDP) of this area is 22 per cent of the total GDP of Indonesia. In addition, 85 per cent of financial institutions workers are located here.

Observing Jakarta as a lone entity is interesting. A number of observers and critics say that Jakarta – which has a total administrative area of 661.52 km² – is not a city, but a large village, or a *village-city*. This is due to the fact that the area now known as Jakarta began as villages that have still survived today. When one reaches Jakarta by air, or sees Jakarta from the height of a building, or even from a flyover,

one would see that the ground is completely covered with the roofs of houses (which are generally terracotta): dense, chaotic, without well-planned infrastructure. It was the Dutch who first built a complete city with well-planned infrastructure and facilities in Jakarta Kota, close to the Sunda Kelapa harbour. After the citadel was opened the Gajah Mada and Hayam Wuruk roads were constructed, followed by the Menteng area which was designed by the architects P.J.S Moojen and F.J. Kubatz. Post-independence, the first President of Indonesia, Soekarno, moved the centre of the city further inland from Kota (near the harbour) to the area renamed Merdeka Square. He accomplished this by erecting the Monumen Nasional (Monas) on the spot appointed as the zero point of Jakarta. Jendral Sudirman Street and M. H. Thamrin Street thus became the widest and grandest roads of that time. Soekarno, who was a graduate of the Civil Engineering Department of the Bandung Institute of Technology (at that time the Architecture Department was non-existent, which meant that architecture was included in the Civil Engineering Department), fully understood the role of the physical appearance of a city. Therefore, to enhance the magnificence of Jakarta, large-scale structures were built on the areas surrounding Merdeka Square, Jalan M. H. Thamrin, and Jalan Jenderal Sudirman, such as Istiqlal Mosque, the Hotel Indonesia, the Hotel Indonesia roundabout (Bunderan HI), monumental statues, the Semanggi flyover, and the Senayan Sports Centre, which holds a stadium with a capacity of 100,000 persons and remained the largest in Southeast Asia for decades. The plan was concluded with the development of the Kebayoran region: an area designated for large and small houses surrounded by wide streets and neighbourhood parks. The massive developments in Jakarta nearly made Indonesia bankrupt, although they managed to lure migrants from other regions. The first migrants were construction workers, followed by others who slowly filled the roles needed in the newly constructed buildings. When Jakarta was inaugurated as the capital of Indonesia in 1959, the needs for government employees were centralised in Jakarta, causing

Surprisingly, Jakarta – the most crowded city in Southeast Asia – is mostly occupied by rural houses as opposed to high-rises

a population explosion. Later on, Jakarta became the economic centre, in addition to the centre of virtually everything taking place in Indonesia.

This population growth led to a dramatic increase in housing demand. New middle-class housing complexes were developed in Cempaka Putih, Pulo Mas, Tebet, Pejompongan, and in many other areas. Government agencies also built housing complexes to provide homes for their employees. However, the influx of migrants was much quicker than the availability of housing in Jakarta. Therefore, in 1980, with the new regulations regarding housing complex developments, private developers were allowed to open large-sized areas for the establishment of satellite cities in areas around Jakarta, including Bogor, Depok, Tangerang, and Bekasi. For a time these developments were stalled since they attracted small, medium, and large speculators which caused the 1998–2000 economic crisis that hit Indonesia. It was around these years that under the second President Soeharto, the New Order regime was toppled after ruling Indonesia for thirty-two years.

As we mentioned earlier, the development of Jakarta – which had once come to a standstill and was not accompanied by adequate infrastructure or thorough planning – had forced Jabodetabek to merge into a *super area* in which organic pockets grow without observing boundaries. Citizens of Jakarta are used to crossing over these regions and even provinces without having to pass the city centre. For instance, a family living on the outskirts of South Jakarta may prefer to enlist their children in schools in South Tangerang rather than in Jakarta, and those who live on the southern part of East Jakarta tend to shop in Bekasi rather than in Pasar Senen, Central Jakarta. These practices are also supported by the presence of flyovers and highways that connect Jabodetabek.

It is owing to the aforementioned reasons that we decided not to allocate Jakarta to a separate chapter in this architectural guide. Instead, we opted to integrate the capital into its surrounding area – Jabodetabek – to make it easier for readers who wish to visit several architectural works at one time.

The development of middle-income high-rises has not solved the issue of poverty which is in part owing to the influx of low-income migrants to Jakarta who stay on illegal land, such as on the river bed despite floods during the rainy season

Aerial photograph of Greater Jakarta with the peak of Salak Mountain in the background: a rapid population growth in the cities has driven developers to carry out sea reclamation projects as a shortcut, an instant but also unecological solution

The Historical Axis and Identity of Jakarta

Marco Kusumawijaya

The most important *monument* of Jakarta is not one of those to have been erected all over the city, but rather a historical axis stretching from the north to the south, encompassing Sunda Kelapa harbour, Kota, Gajah Mada Street, Hayam Wuruk Street (known during the Dutch Indies government as the Molenvliet), Gambir (formerly Weltevreden) and the Lapangan Monas (or Monas Square, formerly Koningsplein), M. H. Thamrin Street, Jenderal Sudirman Street, and Kebayoran Baru. This axis is profanely remembered (or even forced itself to be remembered) by most – if not all – as the identity of Jakarta. Up until now the axis is still recorded as the most populated and widely travelled area compared to any other road in Jakarta. The axis is thus inevitably encoded into the mental map of the citizens of Jakarta.

However, the understanding of this axis as a monument is not merely profane. There are two other values that support the axis in becoming the most important monument of Jakarta. First, the 15 km monument summarises four centuries of Jakarta's history, complete with the distinctive typology of each period lined along the axis. Each typology is very clear-cut, very different from each other, and represents the history of the period. Jakarta Kota consists of yardless blocks situated right next to roads (most of which began their existence as canals). Pedestrians walking along the pavements can easily stroke the walls of the buildings standing along the roads in this area. This area is the remains of the Dutch East India Company (VOC) from the first half of the seventeenth century, even though there were significant additions during the golden age of the colonial era in both the late nineteenth and early twentieth centuries. One interesting addition in the twentieth century was the building now known as the Bank Mandiri, an art déco building located north of the Stasiun Kota (Jakarta Kota Railway Station). The use of black granite on the floor and walls of the narrow ground floor lobby creates a contrasting and surprising connecting area that leads to the main area on the upper floor: a brightly lit, wide, spacious, and cheerful area adorned with festively patterned maroon Indian marble on the low counter desks (70 cm in height) that enhances the spaciousness of the main area.

Gajah Mada Street and Hayam Wuruk Street marked the *Queen of the East* period, a period of colonial trade consolidation when people felt safe enough to leave the old walled city and were driven by the necessity to open up new land to exploit in the south. The area formerly known as Molenvliet was developed in 1648. Since the beginning of the eighteenth century, the rich had created a trend of moving out of the city by opening and occupying large areas such as Meester, Weltevreden and Tanah Abang. In the early nineteenth century, Gambir (Weltevreden) was officially known as Niew Batavia, which marked the end of the VOC and the beginning of the colonial government (1806). Up until the middle of the nineteenth century, Jakarta seemed to consist of two cities: Oud Batavia (Kota) and Niew Batavia (centred on the Koningsplein, now Lapangan Monas). Both *cities* were connected with the 3-km-long Molenvliet which was hardly developed and consisted of large mansions with huge lawns, such as the house now known as the Gedung Arsip Nasional RI. Oud Batavia was *renaissance* (J.P. Coen was an accountant who studied in Venice), while Niew Batavia was *baroque*.

In the 1920s, Nieuw Gondangdia and Menteng became the sign of modern urban planning, a *garden city* that wholly adopted cars into modern urban planning, or the first real estate that marked economic liberalisation and urban government autonomy. In 1926 Batavia obtained municipal status. Menteng, which originally consisted of Nieuw Gondangdia and Menteng, was one example of modern urban planning in this country. Menteng was developed by the private developer NV de Bouwploeg and headed by the architect P. J. S. Moojen, who also allegedly planned the basic layout of the entire region. The organisation, in the spirit of liberal economy and regional autonomy, managed the planning and physical development of the region, while the municipal government was only involved in land acquisition and providing infrastructure networks.

Menteng and Nieuw Gondangdia were delineated by the drainage canal, now flanked by Sutan Syahrir Street and M. Yamin Street. The detailed plan of Menteng was designed by Kubatz, while Nieuw Gondangdia's detailed plan was compiled by Moojen himself. The two architects' point of reference – and the object that united the two regions – was Jalan Teuku Umar, which formed a strong north-south axis. When Berlage, one of the most important Dutch architects of the time, visited the region in 1931, he commented that in the region »arose an interesting unity«. Two of the most beautiful and important buildings that have marked the northern end of the axis up to the present day are the former office of de Bouwploeg itself (which now functions as the Cut Meutia Mosque) and the Nederlans-Indische Kunstkring building which, for a time, served as the immigration office of Central Jakarta. The importance of these two historical buildings as the determinant of the overall character of the Menteng area is very apparent, even today. This axis is equipped with a roundabout which is adorned with a fountain in the middle. On the southern end is Suropati Park, with a large-sized impressive building that is comparable to the strength of the axis itself: the building now known as the BAPPENAS building. Lines of large plots and mansions found along this axis enhance its status.

Moojen formed unorthodox intersections in Nieuw Gondangdia. This was achieved by designing diagonal and curved roads that intersect or interrupt the north-south parallel roads. The result is an amazing – albeit a bit confusing – array of intersections that creates various corner plots with equally various features. Lembang Park was a technical necessity (a water retention area) which was transformed into one of the most beautiful and functional neighbourhood parks, a statement that still applies today. Kubatz's design is relatively more disciplined. An east-west boulevard (today's Imam Bonjol Street-Pangeran Diponegoro Street) was added as another axis that intersected the Teuku Umar axis at Suropati Park. Another distinctive characteristic of Kubatz's design is the introduction of semi-public open areas in the middle of large blocks, forming unique secondary neighbourhoods. A new type of housing emerged: two-storey houses. These houses were commonly shaped as bungalows or villas, surrounded by gardens and equipped with a front porch. These large houses had marble floors and stained glass windows. Today this bungalow housing typology has all but disappeared, especially along Pangeran Diponegoro Street, where new houses resembling palaces that leave no open space on either side are built.

The area encompassing M. H. Thamrin Street and Jenderal Sudirman Street – with the Hotel Indonesia and Hotel Indonesia roundabout, statues, Senayan

stadium, and Ganefo – emerged during the Sukarno era. Kebayoran Baru, an area situated 8 km from Monas Square which was built in 1949, is a modern urban planning with oriental allusion. It is marked by four boulevards that spread from one centre to the four cardinal points. This is the first urban planning carried out by an Indonesian, Ir. M. Soesilo. Kebayoran Baru integrated large houses with small ones into each block: the larger ones were built on the perimeter of the block, next to the boulevards, and the smaller ones were built on the inside of the block, surrounding the neighbourhood parks. The second value of this axis is its morphological value. Due to its central position, its role as the backbone of Jakarta, and the domination of its spatial form (its large size and length), the axis becomes the most legible and prominent against the overall backdrop of Jakarta. This axis is also the symbol of the continuous mass movement towards the south, to higher grounds where the water is clearer and vegetation abundant. Until today, this move towards the south is still the dream of most Jakartans, even though they realise that it would disrupt the environment.

In the end, rather than making a terrible fuss about the cultural *identity* of Jakarta, why don't we strengthen these historical, morphological, and functional identities? An identity with character is not something that can be taken for granted. It must be continuously formed, actualised, and enhanced not only functionally (for instance, with subway lines), but also artistically and culturally. Identity is not something that is sought and made up, but must be based on the facts or *materials* that are historically and empirically available. There is a wise French saying: »A country cannot build its future without understanding its past.«

Originally published in JAKARTA: Metropolis Tunggang-langgang. *Translated and reprinted with the permission of the author.*

Left and above: Kota Tua (Old Town) was built by the Dutch as the original city of Jakarta and has been nominated for World Heritage Site status by UNESCO

The former Hotel Indonesia (now Kempinski Hotel) was built in the Soekarno era: the hotel's original architecture has been preserved

Overcrowding in Jakarta generates congestion that has become part of city inhabitants' daily life, including those who pass the Welcoming Monument

Faces of Jakarta II: the city's infrastructure does not provide sufficient mass public transport for commuters

Faces of Jakarta II : *the village-city*

Not forgetting their village roots, the majority of Jakartans like to maintain the kampong way of life

Jakarta is attempting to preserve green areas, such as parks, zoos and heritage sites, with the goal to create green open public space that covers 30 per cent of its total area

Realising that a city needs to preserve its heritage, this colonial building in the Menteng area was converted into a restaurant called *Kunstring*

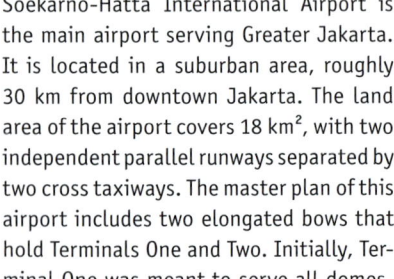

Soekarno-Hatta International Airport

Cengkareng, Tangerang 19120
Paul Andreu
1985

001 A

Soekarno-Hatta International Airport is the main airport serving Greater Jakarta. It is located in a suburban area, roughly 30 km from downtown Jakarta. The land area of the airport covers 18 km², with two independent parallel runways separated by two cross taxiways. The master plan of this airport includes two elongated bows that hold Terminals One and Two. Initially, Terminal One was meant to serve all domestic airlines, while Terminal Two was to accommodate all international flights. Now Terminal Two also serves flights by Garuda Indonesia, Indonesia's national airline. The airport, designed by Paul Andreu, a French architect, was inspired by the traditional plans of villages in Indonesia. Each terminal is equipped with *fingers* that contain clusters of waiting rooms for each gate. The traditional Javanese architectural style, apparent in the roof of each building mass, makes this airport unmistakably Indonesian. In response to the tropical climate of the country, the architect designed half-walled corridors with long eaves. The airport also possesses a very neat tropical landscape design that fills the spaces between gates on each terminal. The landscape of the airport won the Aga Khan Award for Architecture in 1995.

Bina Nusantara University Alam Sutera

002 A

Jalan Alam Sutera Boulevard No. 1, Serpong, Tangerang 15325
Duta Cermat Mandiri
2016 in stages

The Duta Cermat Mandiri (DCM) architectural firm designed the Bina Nusantara (BINUS) University Alam Sutera, a campus university standing on a 50,000 m² area which is capable of holding thirty thousand people. From a distance, the tall building is quite iconic. The architect designed the building as a composition of several blocks with different colours, heights, and measurements. Upon closer inspection, it is revealed that the blocks are the covers of voids whose function it is to create natural air circulation inside the building. The ingenious design plays an important role in reducing the interior temperature and suppressing the use of air conditioning. In addition to the composition of the building masses, the architect also adopts another approach to enhance the expression of the building: different sized ventilations have been placed randomly on to the façade. Additionally, a study on the use of materials and the finishing of the façade – such as glass and cladding – was also conducted.

Sekolah Terpadu Pa Hoa

Jalan Ki Hajar Dewantara No. 1
Serpong, Tangerang 15147
Adi Purnomo
2009

003 A

Sekolah Terpadu Pa Hoa (Patekoan Tiong Hoa Hwe Koan School) is the first Chinese school in Jakarta established during the Dutch colonial era, in 1905. The trilingual national school consists of a kindergarten, an elementary school, a junior high school, and a high school. In the early 1960s, the government stipulated that the students of Sekolah Terpadu Pa Hoa must be citizens of Indonesia. 20 per cent of foreign students were transferred to the school's branch in Blandongan. At the beginning of the New Order era, Pa Hoa Blandongan was closed by the government. In 2008, however, it was reestablished in Summarecon Serpong. The school building was designed by architect Adi Purnomo. On the entrance area, below the signage of Pa Hoa School, the architect designed different sized skylight openings placed at random. As a vertical access inside the building, the architect designed a ramp that is safe for children. On the concrete deck roof, a roof garden has been arranged to reduce the temperature of the room below.

Multimedia Nusantara University Alam Sutra

Jalan Scientia Boulevard, Gading Serpong, Tangerang 15811
Duta Cermat Mandiri
2012

004 A

As with their previous works, the DCM architectural firm has also presented a distinctive characteristic in this particular work: two humongous oval buildings. These buildings, situated in an area of 7,000 m², represent the campus of Multimedia Nusantara University. The larger building consists of eleven floors, including the basement, whereas the smaller one consists of thirteen. On the green roof on the ninth floor, oval voids are scattered all over to allow sunlight to penetrate the building. The architect implemented a sustainable design that saves energy by using two layers of building skins. The outer layer of the skin consists of modular aluminium plates. The surface of these aluminium plates is perforated by pores that act as air vents. Between the aluminium skin and the body of the building is a 70 cm gap for building maintenance purposes.

The modular aluminium panels used for the façade system and green roof are connected by glass, allowing natural light to illuminate the interior space

Bina Nusantara International School

Jalan Lengkong Karya No. 68
Serpong, Tangerang 15320
Duta Cermat Mandiri
2011

The school is an international school located in Greater Jakarta that provides education from kindergarten level to high school in one place. On a site of about 36,000 m², the architect designed a *playground* for students. This is apparent in the configuration of the building masses, which was inspired by Lego®. Building blocks of various sizes are randomly stacked up to three storeys high in which each floor of the building is accessible through ramps and stairways. Each block also displays bright colours, representing the cheerful and lively characteristics of children, as well as eliminating the impression of formality normally conveyed by a school building. Small square windows are spread randomly across the walls of the building, adding aesthetic features to the building and providing fresh air for the interior. In general, the floor plan of the building is designed so as to be oriented towards the grassy lawn and the sports facilities in the middle of the site.

Bakoel Koffie

Jalan Bintaro Utama III Blok AP No. 60, South Tangerang 15221
andramatin
2006

006 A

Bakoel Koffie is a café for local coffee lovers located in one of the suburban areas of Jakarta: Bintaro Jaya. It is positioned right beside the main road, making the café easily accessible to those using public vehicles. The building consists of a single floor with a mezzanine, accessible from the inside by way of a staircase or from the outside by way of a ramp. The architect, Andra Matin, designed the steel-structured building as an open plan building that eliminates interior partitions. As with the Dia.Lo.Gue gallery building, he designed a grille made with wooden boards that serves as both an air vent and a decorative element for the wall that faces the main road. Through this grille, fresh air flows freely into the building, negating the need for air conditioning. Besides the wall, wood is also applied to the fence that borders the mezzanine and the outdoor ramp.

Talavera Office Park
Jalan T. B. Simatupang
Kav. 22-26, South Jakarta 12430
Airmas Asri
2013

007 A

The business and office areas in crowded Central Jakarta are slowly moving to the south side of the city. One such area is along the Jalan T. B. Simatupang, with Talavera Office Park being one of the office building complexes erected here. The office complex consists of two building masses: the Talavera Tower, the main building which was built in 2007, and the Talavera Suites built in 2013. The two building masses are connected with an open area on the podium level. Situated right next to a main thoroughfare and a toll road, Talavera Tower was designed as a landmark that can be easily recognised – even at high speed. The top of the twenty-four-storey building was designed with nine arches that resemble a harp. Talavera Office Park also supports green living by dedicating 80 per cent of its total area to a landscape and open area, a move that is expected to become the standard for other office buildings in Jakarta.

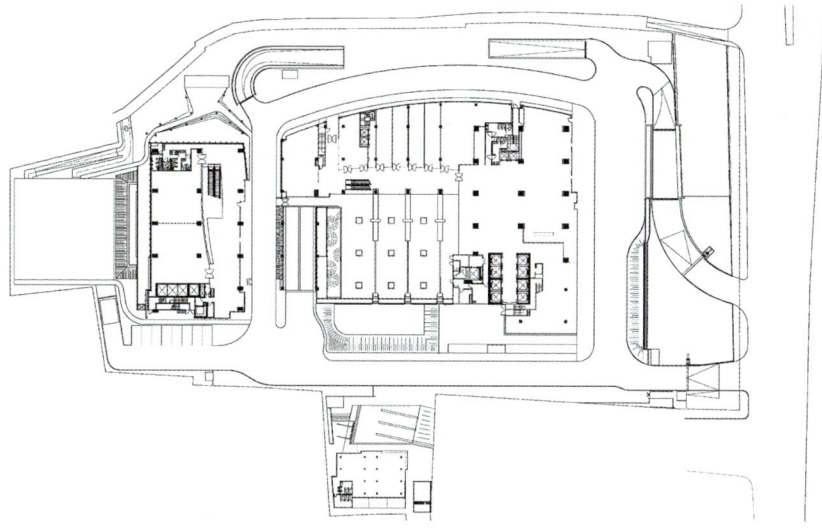

Gedung Yohanes, the Church of St. John the Evangelist

Jalan Melawai Raya 197
Kebayoran, South Jakarta 12130
Han Awal & Partners
2015

008 A

Gedung Yohanes is an extension of the Catholic Church of Saint John the Evangelist Parish, located across from the old church building currently reserved for services. This building accommodates functions that support the parish, such as living quarters for pastors, a meeting room, a chapel, an auditorium, the Grotto of Mary, and a much larger parking space. These areas are connected with extensive corridors and voids that let sunlight penetrate from the rooftop all the way to the basement. In response to the presence of a church, Ayodya Park, and the tall buildings around it, the building takes a silent approach. It was designed as a two-storey building so as not to dominate the area, but rather to synergise with its environmental context and the church. The church itself was designed as a building dominated by brick, creating a sawtooth façade that directs the windows on each segment towards the service building.

ASEAN Secretariat

Jalan Sisingamangaraja No. 70A
South Jakarta 12110
Soejoedi Wirjoatmodjo
1981

The ASEAN Secretariat building is situated at the intersection of Jalan Sisingamangaraja, overlooking the CSW (Centrale Stichting Wederopbouw) roundabout. The building is situated right across from the Perum Arthayasa housing complex, the High Prosecutor's office, and the office of the National Electric Company (PLN) in Kebayoran Baru. The composition of the ASEAN Secretariat's building mass is inspired by terraced rice fields commonly found in all ASEAN member countries. This building also represents the logo of ASEAN, a bundle of rice plants symbolising the stability, peace, unity, and dynamics of ASEAN. The architect responded to the CSW roundabout by creating an L-shaped building that allows visitors to arrive from the direction of Jalan Sisingamangaraja and the CSW roundabout itself. The building consists of nine storeys, with the first four floors serving as the podium. The podium itself is made of an uneven stack of two masses, whereby one of its vertical sides is tilted. On the podium stands a stack of masses whose positions become further withdrawn as they reach the top. The architect placed transparent glass between the massive masses. The podium and the bend in the stacked masses create an angle that has its vertex at the centre of the CSW roundabout.

A

Graha Niaga

Jalan Jend. Sudirman No. 58
South Jakarta 12190
Wiratman & Associates
1992

010 A

Graha Niaga is located in the Sudirman Central Business District (SCBD). The owner of the building wanted the Graha Niaga to be designed by a world-renowned architect. The owner then assigned Wiratman & Associates, a high-rise building structure consultant, to select several distinguished architects from the United States of America. Through a sort of bidding system, KPF (Kohn Pedersen Fox), an American architectural firm which has won a number of world-class awards for high-rise buildings, was chosen. The tower consists of thirty-three storeys and four layers of basement. As a response to its immediate surroundings, the architect gives different touches to each side of its façade. Tropical architecture also became one consideration, and is apparent in the application of sun shading on the entire surface of the building. It was through Graha Niaga that Wiratman & Associates introduced solder piles as a structure to retain the basement walls.

Sequis Centre
Jalan Jend. Sudirman 71
Senayan, South Jakarta 12190
UK architect
1979

At first glance, this twelve-storey office building looks like it is covered with a honeycomb. The sun shading that envelops the entire building is made of GRC (glass reinforced cement), a material used in Indonesia since 1978. The use of sun shading on the entire surface of the building makes it an energy-saving skyscraper.

Gelora Bung Karno Main Stadium

Jalan Pintu V-VI Lingkar Senayan
South Jakarta 10270
F. Silaban
1962

The stadium is part of the Gelora Bung Karno Sports Complex built in preparation for the 1962 Asian Games, hosted by Indonesia. The stadium, boasting a seating capacity of eighty thousand, is designed with a *temu gelang* (joined ring) steel roof structure in circular configuration. It is also equipped with indoor sports facilities and open plazas on the east and west sides. Gelora Bung Karno Sports Complex is one of the Nation Building projects that was initiated by the first President of Indonesia, Ir. Soekarno, in the 1960s.

A

Manhattan Hotel »   013 A
Jalan Prof. Dr. Satrio Casablanca
Kuningan, South Jakarta 12950
Duta Cermat Mandiri
2005

The hotel business is located right in the heart of the Golden Triangle area (Kawasan Segitiga Emas) in southern Jakarta. The proportion ratio of 1:5 between the width and height of the building brings out the bold skyscraper's appearance. On the whole, the composition of the glass cube located on top of DCM's skyscraper is the main contributor to the *wow factor* of this 125-m-high building.

Bakrie Tower » ≽   014 A
Jalan H. R. Rasuna Said
Kuningan, South Jakarta 12940
*H. O. K Architect & Urbane
Indonesia as local architect*
2005

Bakrie Tower is part of the Rasuna Epicentrum superblock and functions as a commercial office building. Standing at 214 m tall, the building consists of fifty floors. The typical floor plan of a tower building was twisted bit by bit to create a tower that is curved like a dress. The slanted and bent columns are designed to conform to the design of this tower. Instead of acting as columns that transfer the load, the structural consultant Prof. Dr. Ir. Wiratman explained that these slanted columns act as the bracings of the building. Around eight thousand façade panels made of glass are applied to its skin. Like the slanted columns, these panels are also adjusted to the curves of the building and thus have different sizes. Bakrie Tower may be the first *organic* tower in Indonesia whose appearance provides a fresh face for Jakarta, whose landscape is filled with box-shaped high-rise buildings.

Dia.Lo.Gue Artspace
Jalan Kemang Selatan No. 99A
South Jakarta 12730
andramatin
1998

015 A

With cultural events and art exhibitions being performed at regular intervals, Dia.Lo.Gue is one of the most-visited art spaces in Jakarta today. Initially, the building served as a graphic design office owned by Hermawan Tanzil before it was developed into an art space open to the public. The building consists of two floors: the first floor accommodates the gift shop, café, and gallery, while the second floor features the office area. The thin stairway made of steel that leads to the second floor is the distinctive characteristic of this art space. In the centre and back area lies the main function of the building: the gallery. The gallery at the back of the building was specially designed to respond to the tropical climate by eliminating massive walls and only applying rotating doors that are almost always open for ventilation. Fresh air also flows through the gaps between the wooden slats arranged horizontally. Dia.Lo.Gue is an oasis that quenches Indonesia's thirst for public art spaces.

The Papilion
Jalan Kemang Raya No. 45AA
South Jakarta 12730
d-associates
2007

016 A

Located at around 10 km from downtown Jakarta, Kemang is a densely populated area filled with residential and commercial buildings. Kemang is also popular among expatriates. Standing by the side of Jalan Kemang Raya, on an area covering 6,000 m², is the Papilion. This boutique mall stands out from its immediate surroundings due to its unique shape: a four-storey-high transparent glass box. The glass panels on this building are supported by steel structure frames and fastened with spider glass fittings which were a novelty at the time this mall was built. The surface of the glass panels are adorned with white butterfly decals. Inside, the Papilion accommodates a restaurant, salon, home décor shop, and a boutique targeting upscale guests. Glass ceilings make the interior of this boutique mall – sometimes used as a temporary gallery – constantly bright and spacious.

Kemang 89

Jalan Kemang Raya No. 89
South Jakarta 12720
Tan Tjiang Ay
2011

Kemang 89 is designed as a multifunctional building that accommodates commercial functions – with the concept of *slow shopping* – and an office equipped with a café. Architect Tan Tjiang Ay designed a large mass block with minimal openings on the side. The transparent mass block of glass behind it constitutes another notable feature of his open-plan layout.

Komunitas Salihara ⌄

Jalan Salihara No. 16
South Jakarta 12520
Marco Kusumawijaya
2008

The Komunitas Salihara complex stands on a housing area covering 3,800 m². Since 8 August 2008, the Komunitas Salihara complex has been the first multidisciplinary art centre in Indonesia which is not owned by either the central government, regional government, or a foreign embassy. Komunitas Salihara was established by arts and culture activists from various professional backgrounds – i.e. artists, writers, and journalists. The master plan of this complex was designed by Marco Kusumawijaya and consists of four buildings: Teater Salihara, Galeri Salihara, an office, and Anjung Salihara. Komunitas Salihara routinely organises arts and culture activities and discussions. The Komunitas Salihara complex has also received numerous awards such as the Best Art Space (2010) by *Time Out Jakarta Magazine*, and was further described as exhibiting »Architecture which applies environmentally friendly aspects« by the Green Design Award 2009.

Salihara Office »

Jalan Salihara No. 16
South Jakarta 12520
andramatin
2008

The office building for the Salihara complex is located on the south side of the site. The building consists of four storeys and one basement. The two upper storeys are used as the office of the curators and management, while the storeys below accommodate the souvenir shop, library, and visitors' toilet. The basement contains accommodation for artists. On the lower floor, Gerai Salihara souvenir shop displays and sells a variety of merchandise of artists who have exhibited their works in the gallery, and the library contains an extensive collection of books as well as providing storage for the data of all artistic programmes ever held in the Salihara complex. The design – which pays special attention to Indonesia's tropical climate – focuses on optimising natural lighting and aeration. This is achieved by creating voids and skylights to reduce the use of artificial lighting, and by the custom-designed filigree applied on the outer side of the building which reduces the penetration of direct sunlight.

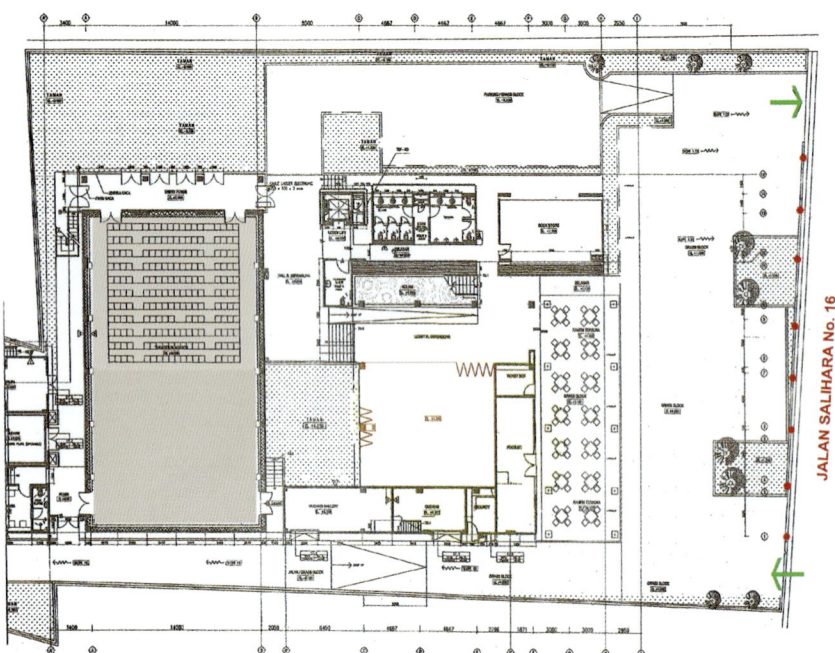

Anjung Salihara
Jalan Salihara No. 16
South Jakarta 12520
Studiodasar
2013

Anjung Salihara was built after the three other buildings in the complex were completed. This building is a pavilion that provides studio facilities for regular practice sessions, guest rooms for performers, and a rooftop amphitheatre. The narrow buildable area forced the architect to develop the building vertically up to five floors. The building has curved corners and was built mainly with concrete – in keeping with other buildings in the Salihara complex.

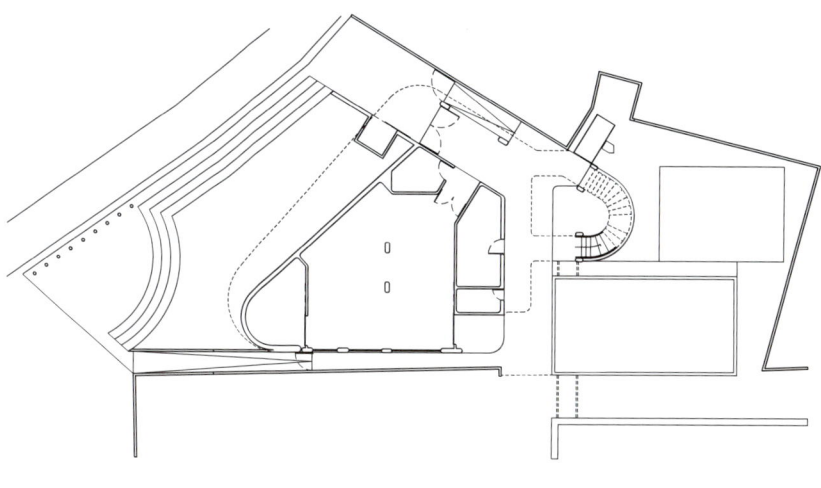

Galeri Salihara

Jalan Salihara No. 16
South Jakarta 12520
Marco Kusumawijaya
2008

021 A

Galeri Salihara is part of the Salihara community complex, located on the front side of the site. As a gallery building, comfort, security, air conditioning and lighting take utmost priority. The gallery area is located on the upper floor. This is oval-shaped and quite large in order to display artworks, as well as being very flexible for any layout concept and installation exhibitions. A concrete floor and white walls were chosen so as not to steal the attention of visitors from the artworks displayed within. The gallery is equipped with an air conditioning system to anticipate changes in temperature and humidity that may affect the quality of artworks on display. On the ground floor are the open Kedai Salihara and the Serambi Salihara, which is enclosed in large glass doors and windows, maximising the penetration of sunlight and natural air circulation.

Teater Salihara
Jalan Salihara No. 16
South Jakarta 12520
Adi Purnomo
2008

Teater Salihara is located on the eastern side of the site, right behind the Salihara complex, and is able to accommodate 252 people. Designed as a black box theatre, the inner walls of Teater Salihara are painted completely in black. The seats can be detached, so that the theatre is flexible for any kind of shows that demand varied lighting and seating arrangements. Soundproofing is paramount to a theatre. To achieve sound proof interiors, architect Adi Purnomo covered the concrete walls with brick, a material that is highly responsive to sound. These bricks are arranged horizontally at the lower side of the walls to reflect sound. Otherwise, they are rotated as much as five degrees to capture sounds from any direction which are reflected and absorbed. The roof of the theatre building is used as an open air theatre called Teater Atap (Roof Theatre). The floor of this area – which is the roof of the theatre building – is covered in grassy lawn that absorbs rain water and maintains a comfortable temperature for the interior of the theatre. This open-air space is designed to accommodate gatherings, jazz performances, and film screenings.

A

West One Marketing Office

West One City, Jalan Daan Mogot
West Jakarta 11460
Studio TonTon
2011

023 A

This building is the marketing office of a mixed-use complex currently being developed in West Jakarta. The distinctive characteristic of this building is the configuration of the triangular roof that is slanted all the way to the ground. The striking roof shields the interior functions which are mostly designed as open areas. Besides the roof, triangular shapes are also visible in the skylight on the roof, the pond, and the ceiling.

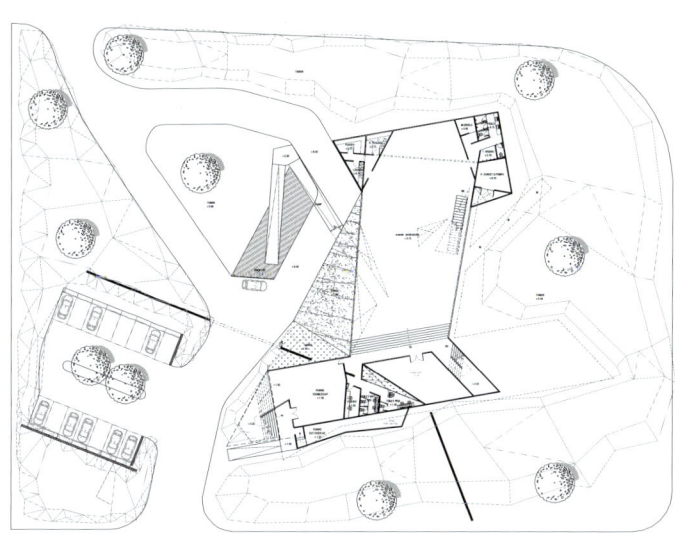

A

The striking triangular roof shields open spaces inside the building

Omah Architecture Library
Jalan Pulau Ayer 2 No. 1
West Jakarta 11610
Realrich Sjarief
2014

Omah Architecture Library is dedicated to practitioners, students, and lovers of architecture by Realrich Sjarief. The library is located on the same site as the architectural firm Realrich Architecture Workshop (RAW), Realrich Sjarief's own architectural firm. The library building is made of wooden frames, with its roof shaped as an arch. Even though the area occupied by this library measures no larger than 30 m², the architect endeavored to make this architecture library available to the public. More than just a library, the place is often used for many informal events by architectural communities. Short courses and an architectural scholarship promoted by Omah Architecture Library are also available. The library is available to visit on Saturdays and Sundays from 10 a.m. to 4 p.m. On weekdays the library is only open by reservation through RAW Architects.

Café Batavia ⌃ 025 A
Jalan Pintu Besar Utara No. 14
West Jakarta 11230
Unknown Architect
1950

The construction of this 165-year-old building lasted quite a long time, from 1805–1850. Before it was converted into a café in 1993, this Dutch colonial-style building was used as a residence, VOC administrative offices and an art gallery. Café Batavia has now become one of the must-visit attractions in Jakarta Old Town.

Historical Museum of Jakarta ⌄ 026 A
Jalan Taman Fatahillah No. 1
Jakarta Barat, Jakarta 11110
Restoration: Boy Bhirawa
2011

The building was built in 1707, before it was designated as the city hall by J. W. Van der Velde three years later. In 1974, the historical building was turned into the Historical Museum of Jakarta. Over time, some restorations and renovations were implemented by architect Boy Bhirawa and his team in an effort to preserve the museum.

Museum of Bank Indonesia
Jalan Pintu Besar Utara No. 4
Jakarta Barat 11110
Restoration: Han Awal
2007

Built in 1828, the building now housing the Museum of Bank Indonesia was the first branch of De Javasche Bank. The building was designed by the famous Dutch architect, Eduard Cuypers, who often included Indonesian architectural elements in his designs. The architecture of this building puts emphasis on the neoclassical style influenced by local (Indische) culture. Han Awal, a conservator-restorer architect, restored the building by tracing the construction method of its time. Seeing that the existing tower was so heavy that it pushed the structure down, it was decided that the tower must be disassembled and the foundation supported with lightweight pumice stones. Today, the historical building is known as the Museum of Bank Indonesia, and is reachable by foot from the Jakarta Kota Railway Station. The museum is equipped with an audio-visual feature that explains the history of trade in Indonesia since the pre-colonial era. Museum of Bank Indonesia is open every day except Monday and national holidays.

The building restoration succeeded in emphasising its neoclassical architectural style which is influenced by Indische culture

Bank Mandiri Museum

Jalan Lapangan Stasiun No. 1
Jakarta 11110
J.J.J. de Bruyn
2007

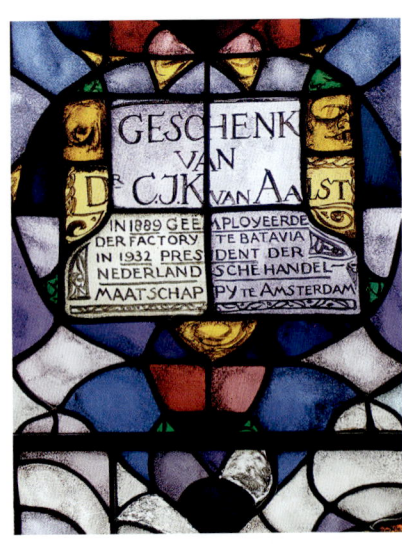

Bank Mandiri Museum was originally a branch office of NHM, or Netherlands Trading Corporation, and was designed by J.J.J. de Bruyn, A. P. Smits and C. Van de Linde. The museum exhibits the bank's space and operating equipment in the colonial era, evidenced by the room storing the *kluis* (safe deposit box), the Chinese cashier room, and the ledgers, security, etc. This art déco bank was launched as a museum in October 1998.

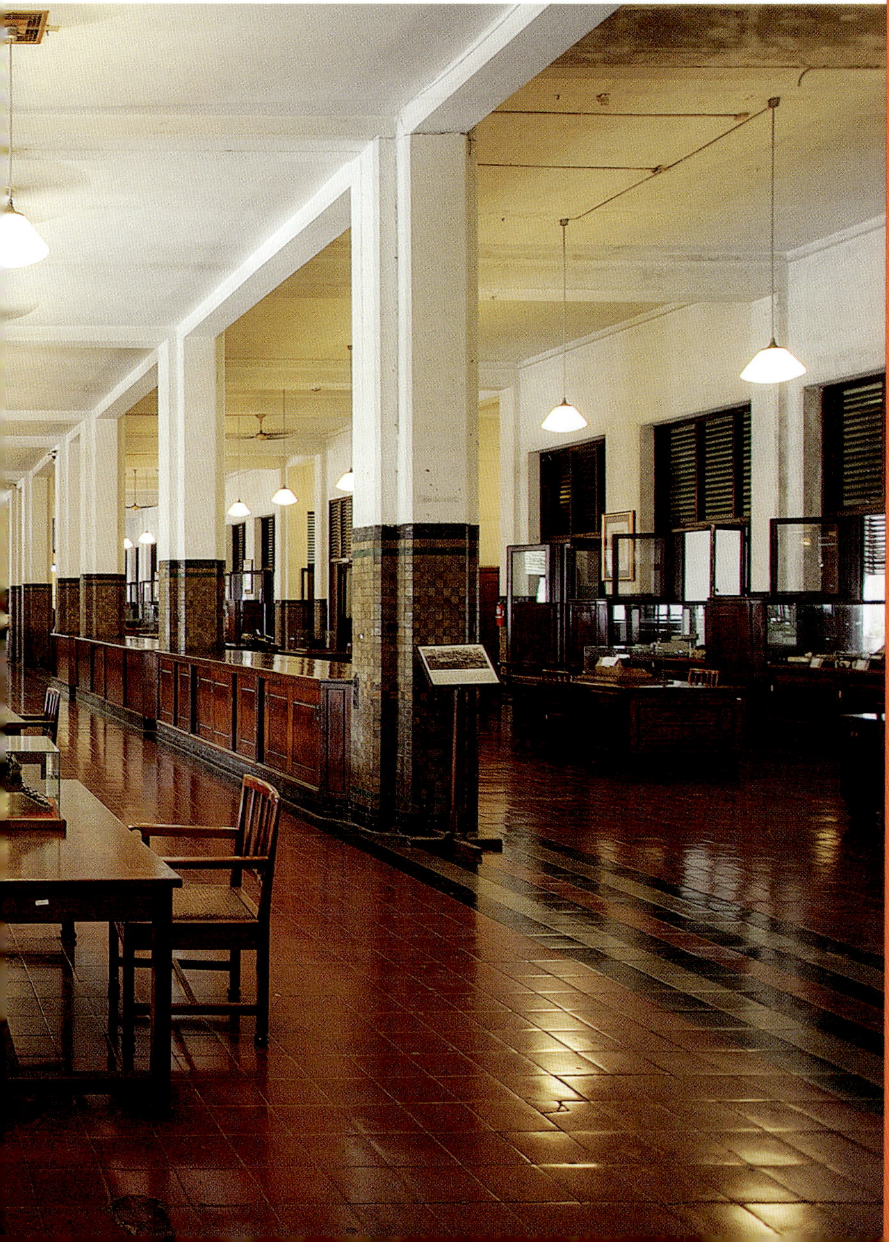

Interior of Bank Mandiri Museum

Gedung Arsip Nasional

Jalan Gajah Mada No. 111
West Jakarta 11140
Restoration : Han Awal, Budi Lim
1760

029 A

During the Dutch colonial era, the building was used as the home to the Governor-General of the Dutch East Indies, Reinier de Klerck. At first, the building served as the headquarters of the Ministry of Mines of the Dutch Indies government, then it was used as the Lands Archief (national archives) building. Following the independence of Indonesia, the building is now known as the Gedung Arsip Nasional. In the year 1992, the National Archives of Indonesia was moved into a newer building on Jalan Ampera. Architects Han Awal, Budi Lim and Cor Passchier restored this heritage building by tracing its history. On the rear building, reconstruction was based on the data of the building after the year 1905. The addition of safety functions, such as fire exits, became one of the most important points. Additionally, the inner court was levelled to accommodate various functions. Today the building and its garden are often used as the venue for weddings, gatherings, and other events.

Stella Maris Catholic Church
Jalan Taman Pluit Permai No. 17
North Jakarta 14450
Duta Cermat Mandiri
2012

030 A

Stella Maris Catholic Church is a recent construction that replaces the old church building which was flooded. The church is designed not only to anticipate floods, but also to emphasise its use of natural materials. From the outside, the new church building looks solid with local stone plates on its walls and vines that cover its fences. The stone plates are very tightly arranged, making the building appear as a monolith. Thin vertical windows are spread all over the body of the building to allow natural light. In order to anticipate future risks of flooding, the architect elevated the entire worship area one level above ground, while the ground floor is reserved for a parking area. The interior of the church is dominated by teak wood which has been applied to the walls of the 16-m-high ceiling. The shape of an upturned arc can easily be discerned from the configuration of the balconies on the mezzanine and the shape of the ceiling. The overall capacity of this new church building caters to about 1,100 worshippers.

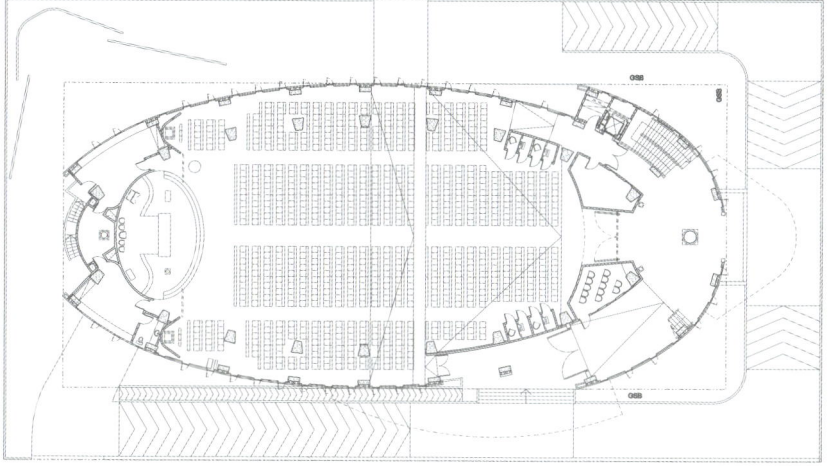

The interior of the church with its 16-m-high ceiling covered in teak wood

DPR/MPR
Parliament Building
Jalan Jenderal Gatot Subroto
No. 6, Central Jakarta 10270
Soejoedi Wirjoatmodjo
1972

031 A

In 1964, at the initiative of President Soekarno, the Minister of the Department of Public Works (PUTL) held a competition for the design of the building to be used at the CONEFO (Conference of New Emerging Forces), an international political assembly for countries categorised by President Soekarno as new emerging forces. The project was halted intermittently when there was a regime change. When it was continued the building was converted into a place where the People's Consultative Assembly (MPR) and the House of Representatives (DPR) work and hold sessions. The CONEFO is arranged in asymmetrical and organic composition. The building mass where the DPR holds its plenary sessions is positioned with its façade facing the entrance, while the secretariat building is placed beside it, parallel to the entrance. This concept was the result of a discussion with a team of designers who compared the concept to the UN Headquarters, where the secretariat building, which is positioned to face the entrance, is better known than the session building, where important world-changing decisions are made. The iconic plenary session building is protected by a dome which is *split* in the middle. The edges are elevated so that the sides which are *cut* meet at one point. The meeting point of the two cuts is connected with an arc structure that pierces the ground right in the middle, providing a structural solution to achieve a wide-span interior without columns. The International Style architectural design is very dominant in this complex, as can be seen in the pure geometric shapes (cubes) which were the main aesthetic inspiration for Soejoedi.

Istiqlal Mosque

Jalan Taman Wijaya Kusuma
Central Jakarta 10710
F. Silaban
1978

Istiqlal Mosque is situated across from Jakarta Cathedral, northeast of the Monumen Nasional. The mosque is not difficult to locate given that it is right next to a main thoroughfare and presents a striking appearance with its gigantic concrete dome and bold geometric expression. Istiqlal Mosque is one of the *lighthouse projects* built during President Soekarno's era in the first two decades of Indonesian independence. The site where the mosque is standing was formerly the site of the Prince Frederick bastion and Wilhelmina Park, built in the Dutch colonial era. Friedrich Silaban, a Protestant, was the architect who designed Istiqlal Mosque. He won the design competition whose team of jury consultants was chaired by Soekarno himself in 1955. The construction of this mosque began in 1961, although it was stalled for several years in the mid-1960s and finished seventeen years later during the New Order administration under President Soeharto. The main mass of the mosque is able to hold around twenty thousand worshippers and has been dubbed the largest mosque in Southeast Asia. Inside the main building mass, twelve five-storey high columns coated with stainless steel support the weight of the concrete dome. Besides the main building mass, the mosque is also equipped with a smaller hall and a tall minaret where the calls for prayer (adhan) are held. The corridors outside the main building mass surround two open areas which can hold an even larger number of worshippers, especially on Islamic holidays, such as Eid al-Fitr and Eid al-Adha. Buildings that are strong enough to withstand the test of time are one of the defining characteristics of F. Silaban. Therefore, concrete – the material that is resistant to earthquakes and able to last for hundreds of years – dominates this massive mosque. The solid and sturdy expression of concrete is also considered a symbol of modernism and the rise of Indonesia after suffering a long period of occupation.

A

Bank Indonesia Thamrin ⌃
Jalan M. H. Thamrin No. 2
Central Jakarta 10350
F. Silaban
1962

033 A

The headquarters of Bank Indonesia in Thamrin is located at the very end of the Jalan M. H. Thamrin corridor, next to the Arjuna Wiwaha roundabout to the southwest of the Monumen Nasional. The bank's building is possessed of the distinctive characteristics of F. Silaban's designs: a solid concrete edifice with apertures on all sides which allow sunlight and fresh air to enter. This is F. Silaban's interpretation of tropical architecture built in the modern era.

National Monument ⌅
Jalan Medan Merdeka
Central Jakarta 10110
Soekarno and Soedarsono
1975

034 A

The Monumen Nasional was built on the Merdeka Square area, the main area designated for *lighthouse projects* initiated by Soekarno, the first President of Indonesia, as part of the Nation Building

projects following the independence of Indonesia. The square is bordered by four main roads: Jalan Medan Merdeka Barat, Jalan Medan Merdeka Timur, Jalan Medan Merdeka Utara, and Jalan Medan Merdeka Selatan. The Monas is situated in the centre of the square that covers 100 ha. No less than three competitions were held to determine the design of this monument, although the three winning designs were not built. In the end, Soekarno, assisted by Soedarsono, created a design reportedly inspired by the shape of *lingga* and *yoni*. With a construction period that lasted from 1961 to 1975, the design was finally realised as the Monas we know today. Monas is designed as a towering landmark akin to the icons of the world's largest cities. The foot of the Monas is shaped like a flat dish and accommodates the Historical Museum of Jakarta. The towering section of the monument stands 132 m tall, adorned with the symbol representing the fire of independence, made of 50 kg gold, at the top. Visitors can climb to the top of Monas using a special elevator and thus treat themselves to a panorama of Jakarta from a breathtaking height.

Kosenda Hotel

Jalan Wahid Hasyim No. 127
Central Jakarta 10240
Studio TonTon
2013

Owned by Ruben Kosenda, Kosenda Hotel can be reached by foot from Tanah Abang market, which is famous for its local produce. The city hotel was designed by Ton-Ton Studio for the architecture; Domisilium Studio for the interior, and Stewart Gan, an Australian restaurateur. On the 518 m² site the architect designed an eight-storey hotel with sixty rooms. The building is not attached to the walls of the buildings on either side. These existing walls are used as the canvas on which murals depicting icons of Jakarta – such as kerak telor vendors, the Monumen Nasional, Kota Train Station, etc. – can be found. Moreover, the nuances of Jakarta in Kosenda Hotel are more palpable with the existence of a restaurant that serves authentic Betawi dishes. The diamond shape of *ketupat* – a dish traditionally served during major holidays – was the inspiration behind the unfinished concrete façade. Diamond shapes are visible on the façade, the fence, and the windows. At night, the diamond-shaped windows morph into glowing eyes which make the hotel easily recognisable. Kosenda Hotel also acts as an exhibition space for local artworks, from the whimsical floor-to-ceiling mural of Jakarta by Sanchia T. Hamidjaja near the entrance, to the paintings by Triyadi Guntur Wiratmo that line the corridors, or the mid-century furniture from Mr. Kosenda's own collection.

Wisma Nusantara

Jalan M. H. Thamrin 59
Central Jakarta 10350
Wiratman Wangsadinata
1973

The building was initially funded by Japanese war reparations. The funds meant to compensate for the Japanese occupation of Indonesia were then used by the first President of Indonesia, Soekarno, to construct a number of *lighthouse projects*, one of which is Wisma Nusantara – the tallest building in Indonesia in the 1970s. When the Japanese war reparations funds were depleted, the government of Indonesia was required to cooperate with the Japanese government. Indonesia's capital included an area reserved for Wisma Nusantara and the construction of the Hotel President. The Japanese government, meanwhile, was required to fund the completion of both construction projects. Wiratman Wangsadinata, a leading figure in the field of civil engineering in Indonesia, was assigned to evaluate the structure of both Wisma Nusantara and the new Hotel President, as well as the financing of both buildings' construction. A steel structure was chosen by Japan, with consideration given to the cost factor since Japan wanted to settle the war reparations funds as quickly as possible. On the other hand, Japan also wanted to build Wisma Nusantara as safely as possible, given that this was the first time

Japan had constructed a tall building. During the construction period, President Soekarno suggested incorporating the element of Garuda spreading its wings into the design of Wisma Nusantara. However, Japanese engineers did not fully accommodate the suggestion. A pair of *wings* on the left and right of the building were designed, but only as ornamentation. Furthermore, the building was used as the prototype in the construction of tall buildings in Japan, since at that time Japan had never actually designed buildings as tall as ten storeys. In other words, Wisma Nusantara was an experimental project for Japan, but also a medium for learning the construction of tall buildings for Indonesian engineers.

A

Hotel Indonesia ⌃   037 A
Jalan M. H. Thamrin No. 1
Central Jakarta 10310
Abel Sorensen
1962

Said Naum Mosque ⌄ »   038 A
Jalan Kebon Kacang 9 No. 25
Central Jakarta 10240
Adhi Moersid
1997

The hotel was opened in the early 1960s to accommodate guests of the state visiting for the 1962 Asian Games which were held in Jakarta. It is located in the main corridor of Jalan M. H. Thamrin, right next to the Bundaran Hotel Indonesia – or the Hotel Indonesia roundabout – where the Tugu Selamat Datang stands. Abel Sorensen, the American architect who designed the hotel, was challenged by Soekarno to respond to Indonesia's tropical climate by applying cross-ventilation principles to this large-scale hotel. Sorensen thus applied balconies typical of tropical buildings. The grid of balconies – a continuation of the hotel rooms' composition – looks neat on the exterior of the building. As the embodiment of the *face* of Indonesia, the interior of the hotel reflects the characteristics of Indonesia through batik elements and works of art created by Indonesian artists. In 2009, the hotel was expanded into Hotel Indonesia Kempinski and was renovated by adding Grand Indonesia as one of the premier shopping centres in Jakarta. Even though this historical hotel has undergone a *change of clothes*, the nuances of the old Hotel Indonesia are maintained through strong horizontal elements on the façade of the building.

The design for this mosque was the winner of the competition held by the government of Jakarta in 1975. Its layout comprises a 400 m square capable of holding around six hundred worshippers. The roof of the mosque is two-tiered, akin to the traditional meru roof. However, the topmost roof is twisted by 45 degrees, creating ventilations that make the building feel cooler, despite it being situated in the middle of a crowded urban area. This mosque was awarded the Aga Khan Award for Architecture in 1986.

Wisma BNI

Jalan Jenderal Sudirman Kav. 1
Central Jakarta 10220
Zeidler Partnership Architects
1996

Wisma BNI is situated within a 16 ha mixed-use functional area in Central Jakarta. Measured from the ground to the very top of the building, Wisma BNI is 262 m tall. The pointed top of the building means the structure is affectionately known as the *fountain pen tower*. Twenty-three high-speed elevators (with a speed of up to 360 m per minute) allow vertical access to the entire tower. The composition of glass on the façade is curved according to the composition of the building mass and is equipped with horizontal windows. Each detail of this building – also known as BNI Tower – was designed in line with international standards by Zeidler Partnership Architects, an architectural firm which has garnered a number of awards for their works. Other works of Zeidler Partnership Architects that have gained worldwide recognition are Canada Place in Vancouver, Canada, and Media Park in Cologne, Germany. Up until today, Wisma BNI is still one of the most recognisable icons of Jakarta's skyline.

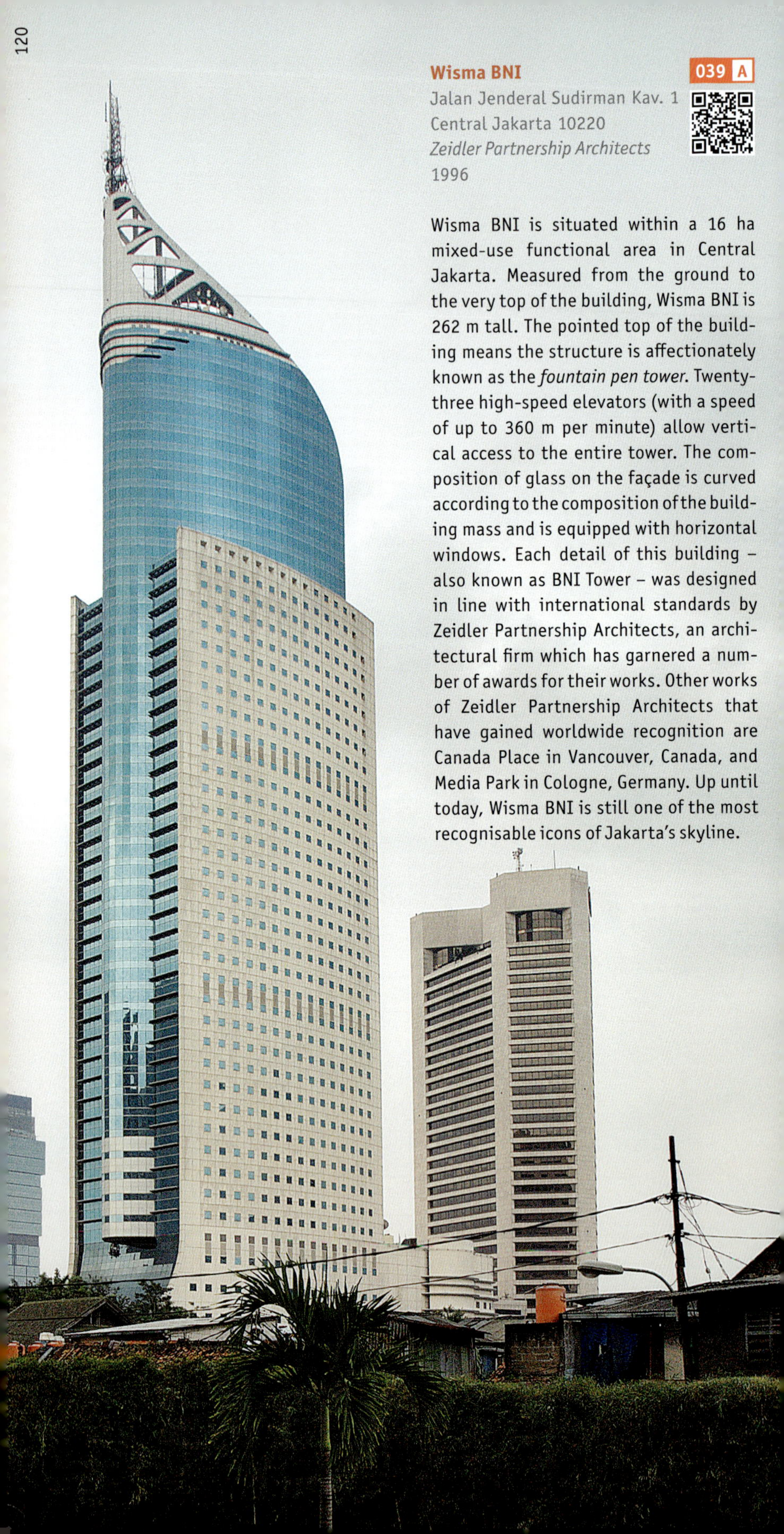

UOB Plaza

Jalan M. H. Thamrin No. 10
Central Jakarta 10230
Duta Cermat Mandiri
2010

This building was initially designed for Westin Hotel. The main idea came from glass blocks arranged overlapping one another. The arrangement of these different sized blocks creates a façade that forms a unique composition. A double-glazed system is applied to the entire façade of the building, except for the podium lobby. This system was applied to reduce energy consumption and insulate heat. A slightly different style of design is visible on the centre of the building mass, as though to give a breather to this asymmetric design. At the top of the building, a vertical plane is inserted to mark the area designated for signage. The *head* of this building also denotes the termination of the skyscraper's design. During the construction process, half of the tower was used as the headquarters of Bank UOB. The design is one of the most iconic buildings to adorn the face of Jakarta.

Wisma Dharmala

Jalan Jenderal Sudirman
Kav. 32, Central Jakarta 10220
Paul Rudolph
1989

041 A

Wisma Dharmala, now known as Intiland Tower, is an office tower located in the premium business area in Jakarta. The white building is quite prominent due to its unique design. Paul Rudolph, the American architect who designed Wisma Dharmala, created a typical floor plan with a basic square shape on all twenty-seven floors of the building. The building is outfitted with stacked saddle roofing on which each stack is twisted 45 degrees. The outermost walls are designed slightly slanted so that the *roof* of each floor serves as the eaves for the floor below. Tropical architecture elements are present in the shape of balconies filled with greenery which circle the building from top to bottom. Twin cylindrical columns made of composite prestressed concrete – applied along the perimeter of the building – serve as the main support structure.

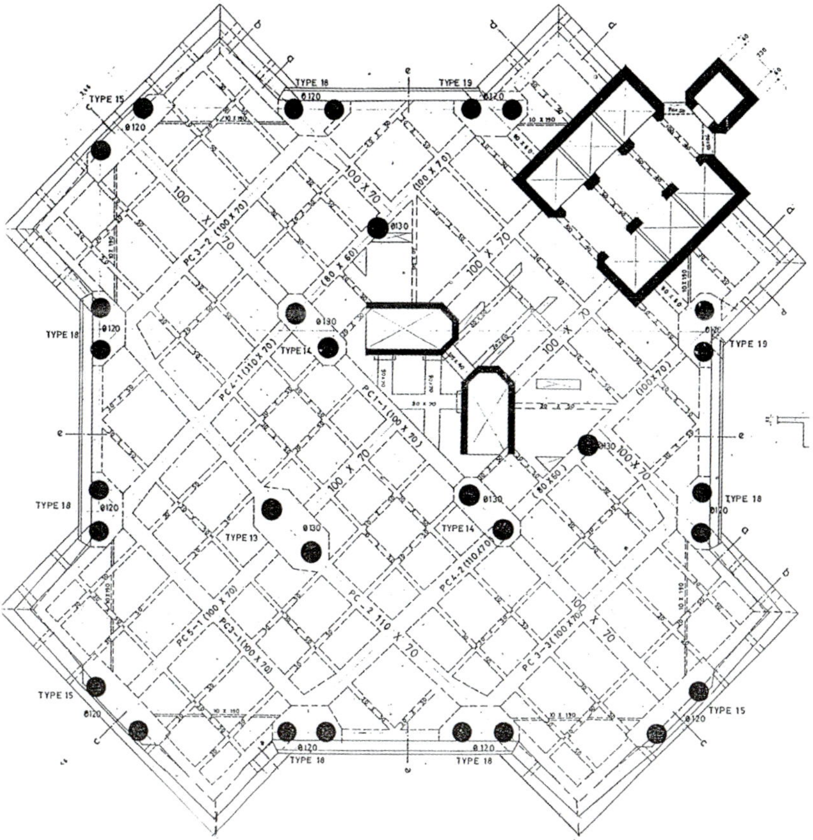

Kampus Semanggi University of Atma Jaya

Jalan Jend. Sudirman 51
Jakarta 12930
Han Awal & Partners Architect
1967

Semanggi Campus, the university's main building, is indisputably one of the post-modern architectural milestones to be found in Indonesia. The building accommodates university functions such as the faculty of social science, engineering, biotechnology, and the postgraduate faculties. The architect Han Awal implemented a second skin system that serves to deflect sunlight from the building.

Metropole Cinema

Jalan Pegangsaan 21, Menteng
Central Jakarta
Liauw Goan Sing
1932. Revitalisation in 1984 and 2008

Bioscoop Metropool (according to the Dutch spelling) is the largest and oldest cinema in Jakarta. In 1993 it was declared an A-class heritage building. This public space is characterised by art déco architecture and targets the upper middle class. It now bears the name of Metropole XXI.

Tugu Kunstkring Paleis (Formerly the Immigration Building)

Jalan Teuku Umar No. 1
Menteng, Central Jakarta 10350
P. A. J. Moojen
2005

The Kuntskring building was built in 1914 by the Dutch architect P.A.J. Moojen. The building is Moojen's second design in Jakarta. The word *Kuntskring* itself means *art society*. In 1936, the building functioned as the office of Majelis Islam A'la Indonesia, and then served as the immigration office. During the New Order era, the historical building was sold and abandoned. Windows, chandeliers, and even stairways were stolen and sold on the black market. The building – in terrible condition – was eventually bought by the municipal government of Jakarta, who assigned architect Arya Abieta to restore it. During the restoration process another function was introduced: the bar. The restoration was carried out by demolishing elements which were not consistent with the original building; returning the building to its original shape and form; replacing lost architectural elements based on research, and adding supporting functions. The building has now been converted into a restaurant.

The Hermitage Hotel

Jalan Cilacap No.1, Menteng
Central Jakarta 10310
KIAT Architects and Thomas Elliott
2014

Located in Menteng, one of the elite areas of Jakarta, The Hermitage is one of Jakarta's historical buildings built during the Dutch colonial era. Initially the building was used as the office of a Dutch telecommunications company, the Telefoongebouw. After changing hands for decades, the building was finally renovated and equipped with both modern facilities and a nine-storey building designed to look as similar as possible to the old building. In 2014 the building was completely renovated by KIAT Architects and Thomas Elliott and was inaugurated under the title of The Hermitage. The hotel offers ninety rooms in six categories. Each room is designed with a colonial ethnic theme. The Hermitage has preserved the art déco style from its façade down to the smallest detail, evidenced in the marble floors, tile keys, and the window and door frames.

Morrissey Hotel

Jalan KH Wahid Hasyim No. 70
Menteng, Central Jakarta 10340
Aboday
2011

Morrissey Hotel is located on an organically shaped flag lot that measures 10,000 m². The hotel is just around the corner from Jalan Jaksa, an area in Jakarta famous for its backpacker accommodation. The hotel's surrounding neighbourhood comprises areas which are awake for twenty-four hours, seven days a week: Menteng, and the central business district of Jakarta. The Aboday Design architectural firm – which designed the hotel with 135 bedrooms, a restaurant, and a meeting room – decided to execute a design approach oriented to an urban lifestyle. The hotel's building mass was divided into two: the front mass (Mass A), and the rear mass (Mass B). The mass located on the front side of the lot consists of five storeys. The small number of storeys is a contextual response to the overcrowded condition of the city that leads one to overlook the human scale. Mass A was deliberately built as a low-rise building to create a pedestrian-friendly scale perspective and a gradation to the skyline of the building as a whole. Window placements, amusing roller blinds and lighting, as well as the use of glass, become the appeal and the distinguishing feature of Mass A compared to the ten-storey Mass B, located right behind it. Unlike Mass A, Mass B (which holds the grand lobby, business centre, and bedrooms) is the antithesis of the transparent building mass in front of it. Typical bedroom windows are designed to be small and are randomly placed. The interior of the room is mostly in white, with a splash of exposed brick for contrast. The façade is designed as a multifaceted wall that irregularly bends inwards, thick on some parts and thin on others. The signature design is the void located on storeys five to eight, with a multilevel bridge traversing the void and facing both the central business district of Jakarta and the Menteng area.

Kementerian Perdagangan Republik Indonesia

Jalan M. I. Ridwan Rais No. 5
Gambir, Central Jakarta 10110
Duta Cermat Mandiri
2008

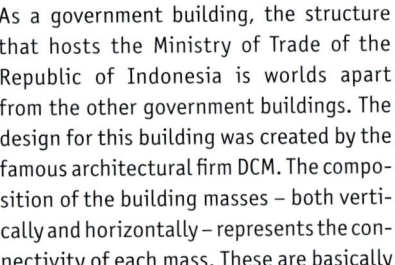

047 A

As a government building, the structure that hosts the Ministry of Trade of the Republic of Indonesia is worlds apart from the other government buildings. The design for this building was created by the famous architectural firm DCM. The composition of the building masses – both vertically and horizontally – represents the connectivity of each mass. These are basically rectangular blocks with different patterns and cladding systems which represent the various neatly packaged services and goods available in the export-import sector. The vertical and horizontal masses are designed connected to each other in order to symbolise relations between the various nations, which are continuously connected by trade. The architect's exploration was not only conducted on the design of the building, but also on its green concept. A large void was designed in order to reduce the temperature of the interior and create shade. Additionally, the lobby is tiered to promote air circulation and reduce the use of air conditioning units.

Hall of the University of Indonesia

University of Indonesia
Depok 16424
Budi A. Sukada
1986

048 A

The building, designed by the architect Budi A. Sukada, is the largest building in the UI campus complex in Depok. The hall traditionally hosts graduation events. The building essentially adopts the form of four large pillars or columns that support the roof. In 2010, the expansion of the hall was turned into a competition won by a student of the Architecture Department of UI. Now the hall is 7,915 m² wide.

Administrative Centre of the University of Indonesia 049 A

University of Indonesia
Depok 16424
Gunawan Tjahjono and team
1986

This building is widely known as the Gedung Rektorat (Rectorate Building) and is the tallest building in the university complex. Standing on an area covering 1 ha, the building consists of nine floors which accommodate several functions, including research institutes and academic administrative services. The most prominent architectural element of this building is the stacked roof, inspired by the traditional meru one.

Central Library of the University of Indonesia
University of Indonesia
Depok 16424
Duta Cermat Mandiri
2011

050 A

The building is located in the middle of the University of Indonesia complex in Depok, West Java. It is adjacent to the Faculty of Computer Science and the mosque, right across from the Faculty of Law. As a public facility, the building is designed to be one of the icons of the campus, easily recognised by visitors. The architect designed the Central Library of the University of Indonesia based upon the concept of a set of stone inscriptions protruding from a green hill in a radial configuration. The building consists of five floors, with only two floors visible from the outside and the rest buried underneath the artificial hill. The artificial hill actually comprises the first, second, and third floors of the building whose roof is designed as a gentle slope covered in greenery to resemble a hill. Floors four and five appear prominently as a set of concrete buildings dominated by black and dark grey. The floor plan of the area inside the hill is circular and centred on the water feature, with the main entrance facing the one and only artificial lake in the university complex. The first floor consists of internet rooms, a cafeteria, and the shop, while the library and reading rooms are located on the second, third, and fourth floors. These functions are reached through a circular ramp that serves as the vertical circulation apparatus. The topmost floor, accommodating the computer room and the thesis defence room, is reached by elevator. While the exterior of the building possesses a dark and stern expression, the interior of the Central Library of the University of Indonesia is much brighter with nuances of light grey and white. The skylights that crisscross the surface of the artificial hill provide enough sunlight, making the whole area well-lit without any indication of it being buried underground. The area above the hill, with its numerous glass applications, is also brightly lit.

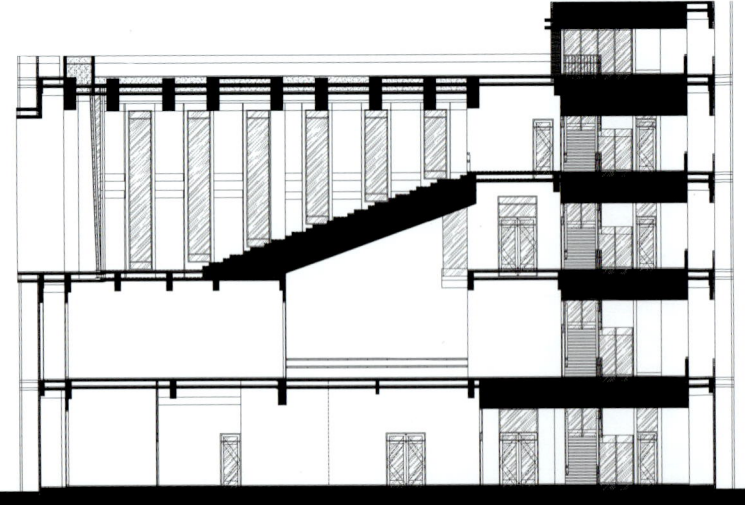

Plaza Quantum Elektro FTUI
University of Indonesia
Depok 16424
Yori Antar
2012

The building was erected to support the research and development of electrical engineering at the University of Indonesia. Located on a 20 m x 30 m site in the Faculty of Engineering complex, the Plaza Quantum Elektro is a five-storey building with a total floor area of 1,700 m². The building's skin is composed of brick with wide openings that allow the building to breathe.

Bogor Raya School
Perumahan Danau Bogor Raya
Bogor 16143
Indra Tata Adilaras
2012

052 A

The part designed by the architect is an extension of the existing building, which was built due to the increasing demand for classrooms. The architect designed a three-storey building in the shape of a white cube adorned with windows of different sizes. The extension building features a double-height library, kindergarten classrooms and common areas.

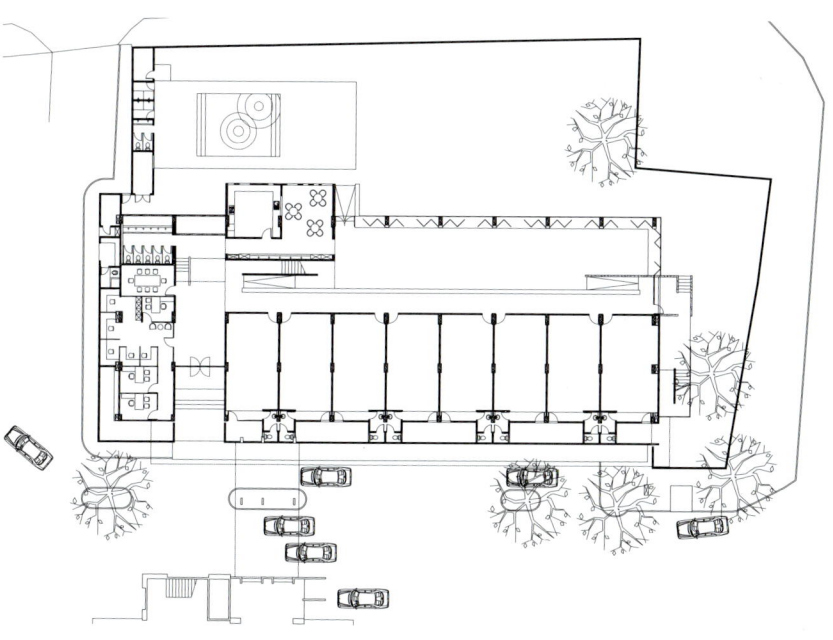

Cikampek Rest Area
Jakarta-Cikampek Toll Road
KM 19, Cikampek 17520
d-associate
2008

053 A

The rest area, located on the side of the highway leading to Cikampek from Jakarta, never fails to grab the attention of drivers. Fuel dispenser units are lined under the strikingly lengthy horizontal roof which is supported by bright red slanted columns. The rest area is the only fuelling station managed by Pertamina whose design is extraordinarily attractive.

Java

SUMATERA

Sunda Strait

BANTEN JABODETABEK

066 064

054

065 057 058 062

WEST JAVA 055 056 061 060 063 CENT JA

059

Indian Ocean

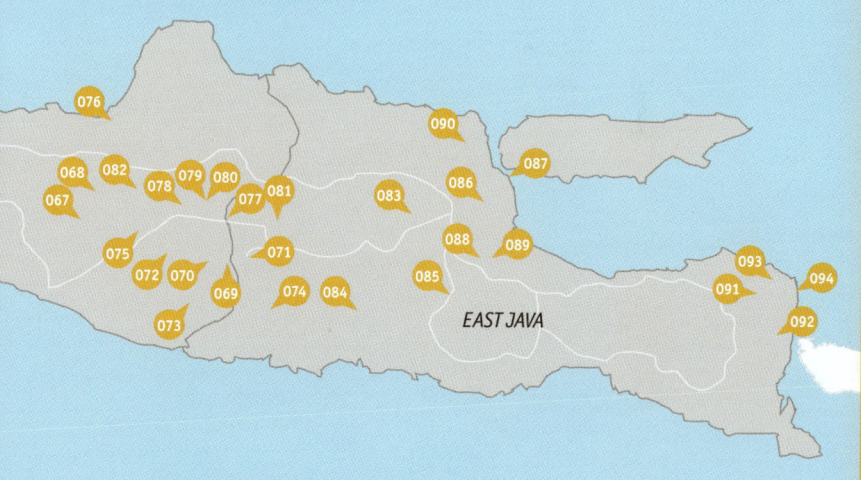

Located in the Ring of Fire, Java Island comprises volcanic mountains, hills, and valleys which provide beautiful and dramatic scenery

Active volcanic mountains on Java Island produce rich and fertile soil across the majority of the land

Java, the Island with a Prodigious History and Super Rapid Development

Imelda Akmal

Java is a special island. It has an extremely long history, and is estimated to be one of the oldest historical places in the world. Its strategic location among calm seas made traders rush to Java from all over the world, especially traders from China and India who were forced to rest and wait for the passing of the west wind before continuing their travels to other parts of the world. Java was also fought

Abundant harvests made Java a rich island in the past; currently, as a result of the housing demand and the burgeoning population, the majority of agricultural land has been replaced by buildings, thus creating a food shortage

over by colonists from Great Britain, the Netherlands and Japan due to its natural potential and abundant crops.

The island is exceedingly beautiful. Java is highly contoured with valleys, cliffs, and mountains. Volcanoes line up along the island, thrusting their peaks into the sky, and often spewing lava containing highly nutritious materials that make the island fertile. Abundant crops have made Java a rich island in the past, which is why its kingdoms were known as the most powerful and prosperous kingdoms in the entire archipelago. Two majestic stone constructions erected in the seventh and eighth centuries, the Borobudur and Prambanan temples, are evidence of that past glory. The first city in Indonesia, Trowulan, was also established in Java during the reign of the Majapahit Empire in East Java. This city was the modern city of its era. In the fourteenth century, Trowulan possessed rigidly defined housing zones and even a sophisticated irrigation system. When the Majapahit Empire went into decline and the Dutch arrived, the Dutch colonial

B

government shaped and established new cities on trade routes that also supported other needs. The government also built roads and railway lines that made trade cities flourish and agrarian towns diminish. The development continued well after Indonesia's independence and now these cities – Jakarta, Semarang, Yogyakarta, Solo, Cirebon, Bandung, amongst others – are Java's largest.

Jakarta was the first city that was built by the Dutch colonial government. It began as a trading port city and has now developed into a metropolitan with no less than eight million inhabitants. Today, Java, whose size is merely 7 per cent of the total area of Indonesia, is inhabited by more than 60 per cent of Indonesia's population. It has thus become the most densely populated island in the world with a population of over 150 million.

This density significantly fuelled the development of construction. Even though Jakarta dominates as the centre of each aspect in Indonesia – namely the economy, politics, and construction – other cities

Borobudur from a distance

are also catching up. This is especially true after the centralised system was abandoned and Indonesia instead implemented a policy of regional autonomy. Cities outside Jakarta have grown significantly over the last ten years, with the acceleration of development being particularly pronounced in Java. The development of new housing complexes and gigantic factories has dislodged the dominance of agricultural fields, transforming the once green island into a single large mass chock full of manmade structures – particularly discernible on the main transport routes or along the regional roads and city nodes.

Freeways are stretched along the island to add to the length of roads and reduce traffic jams that mushroom sporadically across many cities in Java. In many places in Java, the development has spiralled out of control. Furthermore, each regional government is struggling to keep their respective governed area as unique as possible. Bandung, a city well known for its intellectuals and education centres,

is currently driven by the mission to be a creative city through the Bandung Creative City (BCC) programme. Yogyakarta and Solo are continuously trying to maintain their status as cultural cities, considering that in the past these cities were the centre of Javanese culture. In the meantime, Semarang, the seaport city of Central Java, is trying to adapt to its newest function as an industrial city. On the other hand, Surabaya, the second largest city in Indonesia after Jakarta, seems to be struggling hard to catch up with Jakarta to become the second metropolitan of Indonesia. The development of these cities is of course accompanied by the development of their architecture. Bandung, the city closest to Jakarta, attracts the most attention with its ambition to become a creative city. This may be because the first architectural department in Indonesia was established in the Bandung Institute of Technology, followed by the Architecture Department of Parahyangan University. Graduates of both schools have become prominent architects and impacted on the development of Indonesian architecture. The first President of Indonesia, Soekarno, and the current Mayor of Bandung, Ridwan Kamil, were graduates of these schools. Even though most architecture graduates

An old railway built by the Dutch colonial government

from both schools work in Jakarta and have opened their own architectural firms there, Bandung still owns its fair share of potential architects whose progressive works can be seen within the pages of this book. Salman Mosque, designed by the senior architect Achmad Noe'man; Breeze Art Boutique Hotel by Tan Tjiang Ay; Selasar Sunaryo by Baskoro Tedjo, and Al-Irsyad Mosque by Urbane are but small examples of these. We also recommend Yogyakarta, a city in which the works of many potential architects can be examined. Romo Mangun (Y. B. Mangunwijaya), whose social awareness inspired architects of later generations such as Eko Prawoto, is a prominent example of an architect from Yogyakarta. Romo Mangun's thoughts and notions initiated the Architecture for People movement, which includes the post-disaster architecture of Ngibikan Village, or the Rahayu Youth Centre designed by Yuli Kusworo, Effan Adhiwira and Marco Kusumawijaya – an educational facility built with captivating bamboo.

In contrast, Surabaya's desire to become a metropolitan city that accommodates a middle-class lifestyle is becoming steadily apparent. Here we see that architecture can indirectly describe or reflect what is currently happening in the cities of Java.

Infrastructures, including toll roads, were built in order to connect most of Java's cities, such as Jakarta and Bandung

The city of Bandung: the toll road from Jakarta has stimulated a rapidly growing population, while a slow urban planning has created chaotically assembled villages

Faces of the city of Surabaya: copying famous Western buildings has become a popular consumer gimmick to sell properties

Faces of Surabaya and other cities in Java: in its ambition to be *modern*, Surabayan has decided to inappropriately copy some world-famous buildings, while a low-income population continues to maintain the village way of life

Cities such as Yogyakarta have attempted to maintain their indigenous culture through the preservation of heritage architecture

Breeze Art and Boutique Hotel 054 B
Jalan Pondok Hijau Permai
Bandung, West Java 40559
Tan Tjiang Ay
2013

Breeze Art and Boutique Hotel is the result of a combination of a hotel and an art gallery, located in Setiabudi, North Bandung. The concept emerged from the owner's background as an art collector. Architect Tan Tjiang Ay designed this twelve-room hotel with a distinctive characteristic: the use of thin concrete and an emphasis on the sincerity of the material. The building is also designed so as to be close with nature, thus blending the Bandung city breeze and the beauty of flowers with architecture. Staying in the hotel is like staying inside an art gallery where Maestros' masterpieces are exhibited. The hotel exhibits ceramic artwork by the ceramic expert F. Widayanto, paintings authored by the painting maestro Srihadi Soedarsono, and batik artwork by Go Tik Swan Hardjonagoro.

Sensa Hotel
Jalan Cihampelas 160
Bandung, West Java 40131
Duta Cermat Mandiri
2009

Sensa Hotel is located in Cihampelas, a famous shopping area in the heart of Bandung. The hotel is one of the additional building masses of the Nu Ciwalk (Cihampelas Walk) development concept. Sensa Hotel can be seen from the Paspati (Pasteur-Surapati) flyover. DCM designed this hotel with 108 bedrooms, a restaurant, and a spa.

The eye-catching feature of the hotel is the composition of the white linear curve building mass. This composition resembles Art Nouveau architecture simplified to adhere to the principles of modern architecture. Sensa Hotel was designed as a fifteen-storey single building, shaped to resemble the wings of a butterfly with the barest minimum number of corners. In further keeping with this concept, the windows located on the façade of the hotel are designed as broken lines whose corners are pointed, like leaves. This is similar to floral-inspired Art Nouveau architecture.

Nu Ciwalk
Jalan Cihampelas 160
Bandung, West Java 40131
Duta Cermat Mandiri
2004

056 B

Before it was thoroughly developed, the front area of Cihampelas Walk (Ciwalk) appeared not to have been well designed. For instance, many vacant areas were not used fully amd the shopping mall in the centre of the site was the one and only prima donna within the complex. The DCM architectural firm then developed the Nu Ciwalk with an outdoor concept which has now disappeared from Indonesia. The concept was interpreted into a pedestrian walk which connects Jalan Cihampelas with the Nu Ciwalk area. The series of covered walkways continues to the extension of Ciwalk, which can be found when visitors enter the Ciwalk complex. On the extension, pedestrian walkways connect one building to another. These pedestrian accesses are deliberately designed around the existing pine trees and lead to the main building mass located at the centre of the Ciwalk complex.

Concordia

Jalan Kiputih 12, Ciumbuleuit
Bandung, West Java 40142
Ir. Gmeilig Meyling
Additional Functions: Tan Tjiang Ay
1926

Condordia was built in 1957 by a Dutch architect named Ir. Gmeilig Meyling. Initially, the Concordia building and its surrounding area were the result of a government land swap with a group of Dutch and aristocratic locals called the Societeit. Concordia Societeit was renamed Country Club Concordia. At the time, Ir. Soekarno, the first President of Indonesia, proposed changing Concordia's name to something that had a more Indonesian flavour: Bumi Sangkuriang Meeting Hall. Today, Bumi Sangkuriang functions as a hotel. Since Bumi Sangkuriang is a cultural heritage building, no significant changes were made. Even so, some additional building masses to accommodate more hotel rooms were designed and built by the architect Tan Tjiang Ay. These buildings have simply adopted elements of colonial buildings, which is apparent in the modulation and use of decorative concrete blocks. Bumi Sangkuriang, accessible from Jalan Setiabudhi, won Best Practice Heritage Conservation 2009.

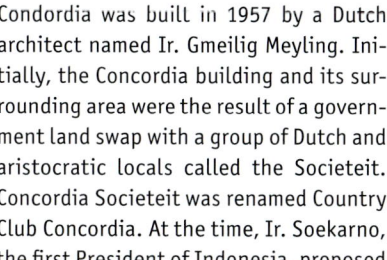

Padma Hotel

Jalan Ranca Bentang 56-58
Bandung, West Java 40142
Kerry Hill
1993

Prior to being renamed Padma, the hotel, which is located in Ciumbuleuit, was formerly known as the Chedi Hotel and in 2000 it was renamed Malya Hotel. Kerry Hill, an Australian architect specialising in hotel design, was responsible for the structure. The architect designated the floor that is level with the ground as the first floor. In a unique twist caused by the fact that the hotel is standing on a hill, floors two to eight are not located above the first floor, but below it.

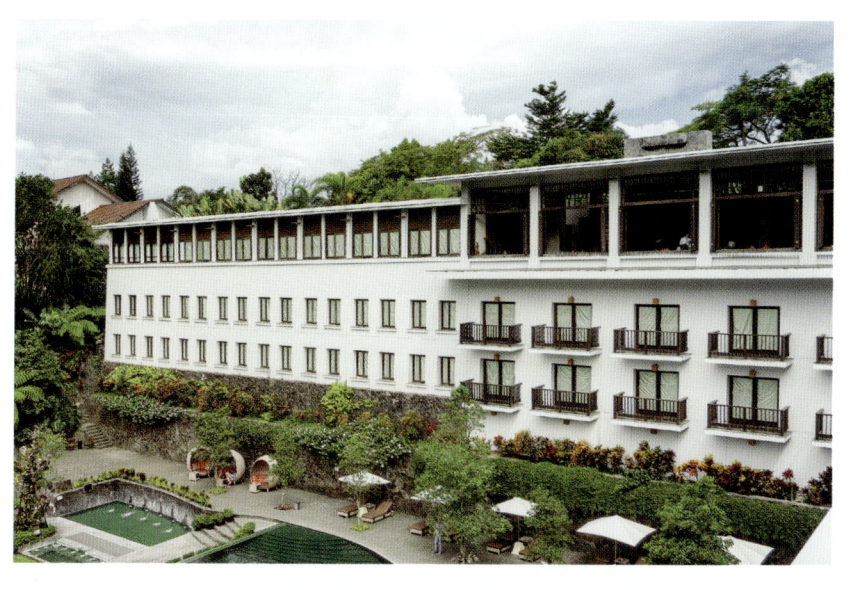

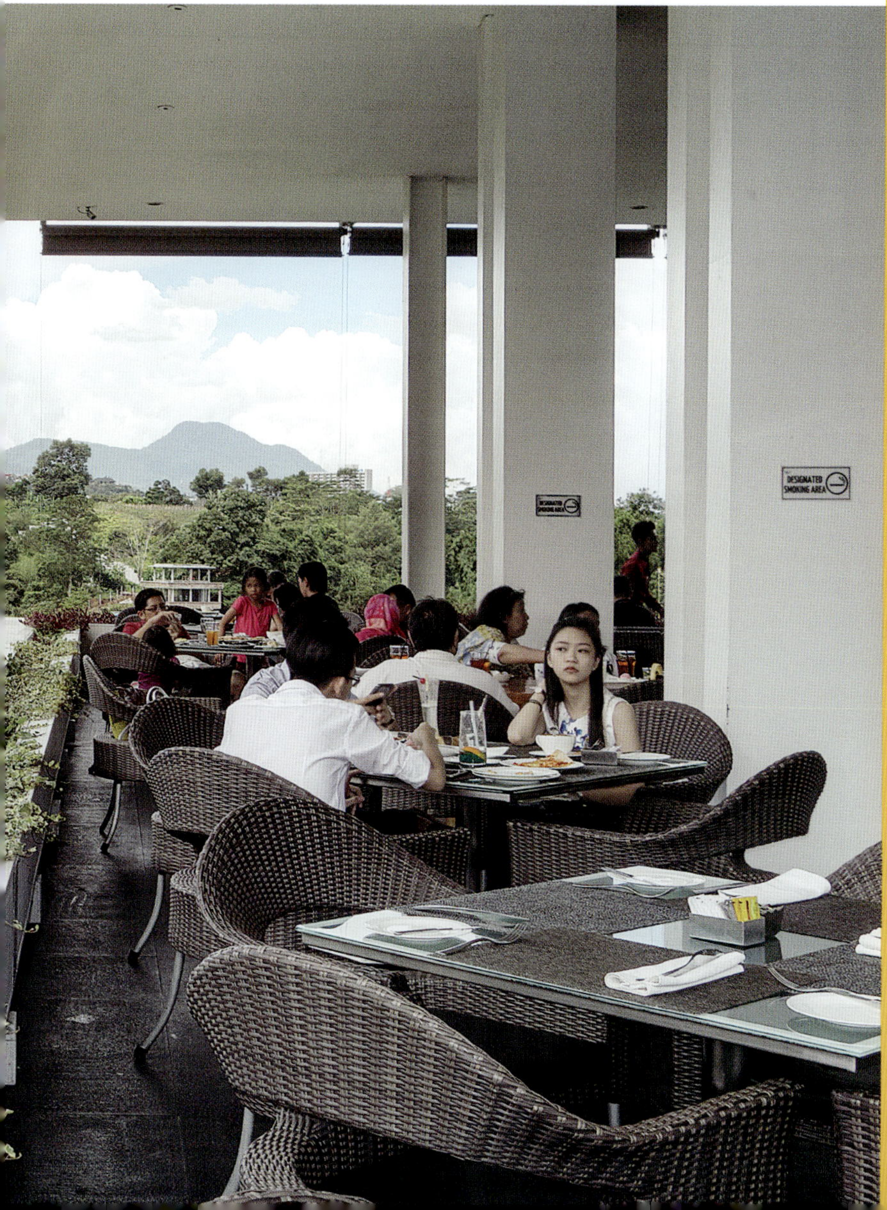
DESIGNATED SMOKING AREA

West and East Halls of ITB

Jalan Ganesha 7
Bandung West Java 40132
Henri Maclaine Pont. Restoration: Bambang Setia Budi and team
2013

059 B

The West Hall (barakgebouw A) and East Hall (barakgebouw B) of the Bandung Institute of Technology (ITB) are well known as buildings with important historical value. ITB, referred to as Technische Hoogeschoolte Bandoeng during the Dutch colonial era, is the first institute of technology in Indonesia that was established during the Dutch Indies era. It is located right across from Salman Mosque, on Jalan Ganesha, Bandung, and is reachable from both Jalan Dago and Jalan Tamansari. The buildings reserved for the halls combine modern architecture and their occidental roots with the geist of local architecture, adapted from Javanese and Batak architecture, as can be seen in the shape of the roof. During construction, the use of laminated wood in the Netherlands reached its height. Therefore, Henri Maclaine Pont, a Dutch architect, chose this material for the roof structure of the West Hall and East Hall of ITB. Sheets of thin laminated wood are glued together and bent to form a wide-spanning arc that serves as the main structure of the building. Triangular modules were created as the base for the roof frame structure because the shape was considered the most rigid. The structure was recognised as a valuable invention and has been used since the colonial era. To preserve the integrity of both halls, in 2013 Bambang Setia Budi and team restored these buildings. The black paint on the structure was scraped to expose and distinguish the laminated wood and steel structure. Usable doors and hinges from the Dutch colonial era were preserved. The drains around the perimeter of the building were moved so that vines could be replanted and climb up to form the head of the columns, just like old times.

Salman Mosque, ITB

Jalan Ganesha 7
Bandung West Java 40132
Achmad Noe'man
1972

060 B

Salman Mosque is the first university mosque in Indonesia. At the time of its construction, the social and political condition of Indonesia was not too kind on mosques, and it was hard to find mosques that stood beside the main road in Bandung, much less in school or university premises. Initially, this mosque was built to accommodate the need for Friday prayers for Moslem students of ITB. The absence of a house of worship was considered a crucial problem. The ITB mosque committee was thus established to fight for their right to build a mosque on an empty plot on Jalan Ganesha. In 1960, the ITB mosque committee sent a proposal to the Rector of ITB and the Mayor of Bandung, but it was rejected. This rejection was because the construction of the office of Lembaga Afiliasi dan Penelitian Industri (LAPI, or The Body for Industrial Research and Affiliation) had already been planned. Requesting an audience with President Soekarno was the next step that was proven to be fruitful and brought good news for Moslem students in ITB. On 30 May 1964, the plan designed by Ir. Achmad Noe'man was approved and signed by Bung Karno himself. The design of Salman Mosque can be considered a milestone for contemporary mosque architecture in Indonesia since the architect designed a concrete mosque without a dome; the dome was instead replaced with a flat roof curved on its four sides. Besides being the *head* of the mosque, the roof – that resembles a bowl – also serves as a gigantic gutter for the flat roof. A prestressed concrete block spanning 25 m in length was used to create a columnless interior. The application of this wide-spanning structure was meant so that the *shaf* (lines) of worshippers would not be interrupted.

Rumah#1 LABO.themori
Bandung, West Java
LABO
2013

The experience of living in Japan has become a defining factor in housing designed by the pair of architects who also own Rumah#1 LABO.themori. Efficiency, such as the application of the wabi-sabi – *living in moderation* – doctrine from the Land of Sakura was the basic approach for the design of this house. The main structure is made with steel, and was built with two and a half floors with a mezzanine. In designing the house, efficiency is tightly guarded by allocating the area of each room as needed. The layout of each room is arranged so that the distance between them can be covered in one or two steps. At 4.5 m x 7.5 m, the second floor hosts quite a number of functions: a kitchen, dining room, living room, bathroom and the son's bedroom. The mezzanine features the living room, daughter's bedroom, closet, and master bedroom. The rest is void. The architects said that designing this compact layout is analogous to making an efficient clothing pattern on a piece of fabric. Visit by appointment only.

Selasar Sunaryo Art Space

Bukit Pakar Timur No. 100
Bandung, West Java 40198
Baskoro Tedjo
1998

Selasar Sunaryo Art Space is located on the slopes of Dago Hills, North Bandung, not far from the city centre. Constructed in four years (1993–1997) and open to the public since September 1998, the building is a result of a collaboration between Sunaryo, a contemporary artist, and Baskoro Tedjo, an architect. The artist wished to create a public space that would also function as an art gallery. At the beginning of the design process, Sunaryo specifically requested three main requirements for the art space: first, the artist wanted the building to be designed so that it would be able to display his artwork; second, he requested that the whole building should use the architectural elements of West Java in its definite representation of the characteristics and identity of his artwork, and third, the art space was to unite the general public with arts and artistic activities in an intimate dialogue. Selasar Sunaryo Art Space was funded by the artist himself, which brought a special kind of burden to the architect Baskoro Tedjo. The architect eventually decided to design a sustainable building with minimal maintenance. The sustainable concept is interpreted as architecture that grows in time, according to the needs of its occupants. The idea of a minimal maintenance building is realised by embellishing the art space with as little detail and decorative elements as possible. Here, the architect deliberately designed the building to be the background of the artwork displayed within it, in order to make the artwork speak louder. The art space is also equipped with a *Ruang Sayap* (wing gallery) which is reserved for exhibiting local and foreign artwork; Bale Tonggoh, a semi-permanent gallery and activity space; Bale Handap, where artists create their works; Stone Garden, an open space used for exhibiting Sunaryo's artwork made of stone; a bamboo house that accommodates artists who wish to stay over; an outdoor café; an amphitheatre; a resource centre, and a garden and contemplation area. Selasar Sunaryo Art Space won the IAI Award in the Cultural Institution category in 2002.

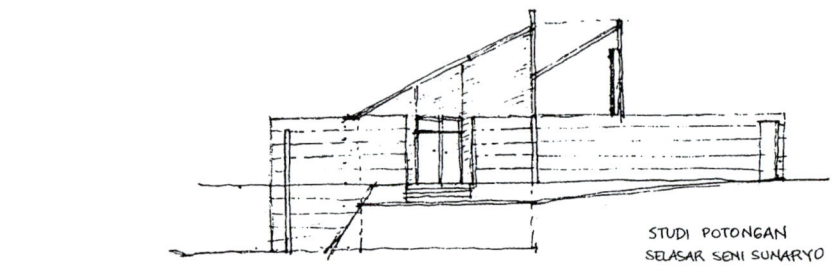

STUDI POTONGAN
SELASAR SENI SUNARYO

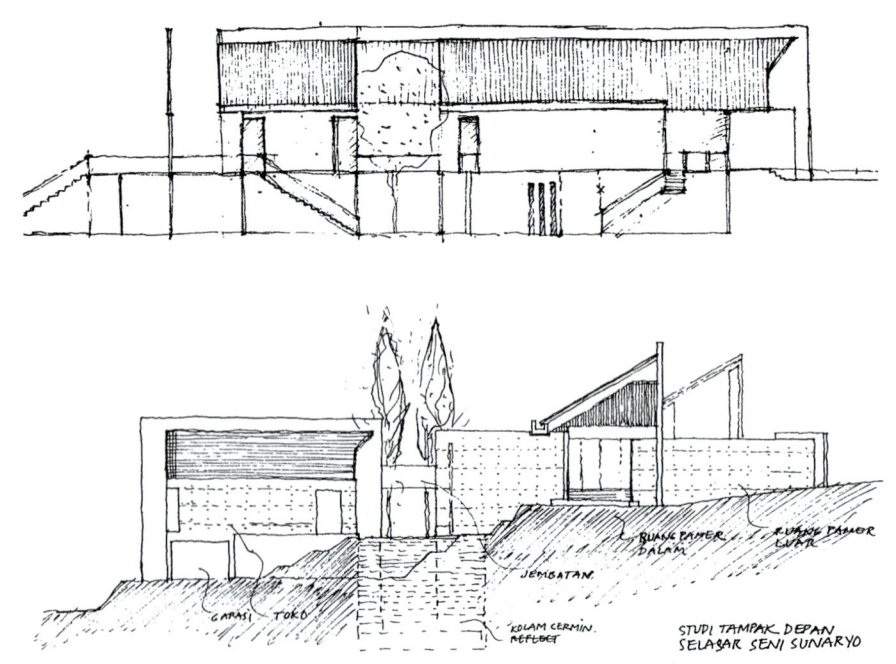

STUDI TAMPAK DEPAN
SELASAR SENI SUNARYO

Gupondoro
Bandung, West Java 40551
Oky Kusprianto
2013

This design represents the architect's experiment with simple physics principles on buildings. The home and studio of architect Oky Kusprianto uses a series of jalousie windows or louver windows for its entire walls. The unique wall design enables the occupants to control their thermal comfort independently since the advantage of these windows lies in their ability to be adjusted. The capacity of the windows' louvers to be opened or closed independently means that jalousie windows can be placed in a list of alternative and effective ways to control natural and comfortable aeration in a building. Perched on the side of a hill in Bandung, the home must automatically familiarise itself with the cool – often cold – climate of the site. During these cold days the louvers are closed. Even so, cold air can still seep through the small gaps between them, thus retaining air circulation and keeping the rooms at a comfortable temperature. The louvers make the house *breathe*. Visit by appointment only.

Dusun Bambu
Jalan Kolonel Masturi KM 11
Situ Lembang, West Bandung
West Java 40551
APTA
2013

Dusun Bambu is a hybrid tourism area that combines Sundanese locality values with modern architecture. The vernacular architectural typology chosen by Dusun Bambu is the house on stilts, inspired by indigenous villages found throughout West Java, such as Kampung Naga, Kampung Ciptagelar, and Kampung Dukuh. This vernacular architecture was then combined with the use of modern materials, such as glass, and a sloping roof. The philosophy of balance in nature adopted from the traditional belief of Sunda Wiwitan is the basic concept behind Dusun Bambu's design. This concept is apparent in the fact that only 10 per cent of the whole area is used as a built area, while the rest is utilised as open green areas. Oky Kusprianto, the principal of the APTA architectural firm, believes that Dusun Bambu is designed as a showcase for Sundanese architecture with a touch of modernity. Sampling meals in the middle of the eucalyptus grove, relaxing in the gazebos, staying over, and performing outdoor activities are some of the pursuits to be enjoyed in this tourist attraction.

Al Irsyad Mosque

Jalan Raya Parahyangan KM 2.7
Kota Baru Parahyangan
Bandung, West Java 40553
Urbane Indonesia
2010

Al Irsyad Mosque is situated on an 8,000 m² area inside a housing complex, not far from the Padaleunyi Toll Road leading from Jakarta to Bandung. Unlike most mosques' typology, Al Irsyad Mosque is a cubical building composed of concrete block modules without a dome. These concrete blocks form the massive walls, while hollow blocks are arranged to form calligraphy on the wall. The single-storey mosque's floor plan is a simple square measuring 28 m x 28 m, and is capable of accommodating one thousand worshippers. The building is oriented to the west (the direction of the Qibla in Mecca), indicated by the mihrab where the imam would lead the prayers. The mihrab area is placed above a serene pool where the architect located a large round stone with the Arabic inscription of Allah. This is to denote the accurate direction of the Qibla. The absence of a permanent wall on the western side of the building allows worshippers to pray facing the verdant valley.

B

Outward Bound Indonesia
Jatiluhur, Purwakarta
West Java 41152
*Andry Widyowijatnoko and
Djoko Kusumowidagdo*
2011

066 B

Located on an area surrounded by mountains in Jatiluhur, West Java, Outward Bound Indonesia is a place that provides training and social activities. The unique feature of this facility is that 9 per cent of the material used for its construction is bamboo. Wood, natural stone and thatch are used as secondary materials. The bamboo used for the construction was taken from the surrounding areas to reduce the energy consumed during the transportation of the materials to the site. The campus complex also features an office, tree house, shelter, tower and hall. The hall within this complex is one of its points of interest. To meet the needs of this wide-spanning and spacious room, the structures are aligned at the top, making the whole construction resemble a leaf or a boat. A 24 m² skylight encircles the top of the structure to allow natural light to flood the interior. The hall was constructed with eight thousand bamboo poles by expert craftsmen and more than 1,000 m² of natural stone was used to cover the floor. The semi-open hall is capable of holding up to eight hundred people.

Amanjiwo Hotel

Majaksingi Village, Borobudur
Magelang, Central Java 56553
Ed Tuttle
1997

067 B

Amanjiwo Hotel lies in the rural heartland of Central Java. The main design of Amanjiwo Hotel originated from Ed Tuttle's homage to Borobudur Temple, located not far from the hotel. The American architect's homage is thus interpreted in circular and square shapes seen in the Borobudur Temple complex. The hotel compound is based upon a radial-concentric design and consists of thirty-six suites oriented towards a gigantic rotunda. This serves as the hotel's *front of house premises*.

Oei Hong Djien Museum

Jalan Jenggolo 14
Magelang, Central Java, 56122
d-associates
2011

068 B

Oei Hong Djien was born in Magelang in 1939. In 1970 he began to collect artworks. Today his collection numbers more than two thousand artworks that include paintings, sculptures, installation arts, and other artistic media. In order to create a home for his collection, he came to the decision to build an art museum, known as the Oei Hong Djien Museum in Magelang.

This small town is around one hour's drive from Adisucipto International Airport, Yogyakarta. At a glance, the façade may look very simple. The building was built facing the main thoroughfare with the entire façade covered in black. The black walls are expected to enhance the works of art on the façade of the building which resemble the reliefs found in temples. The D-Associates architectural firm designed the main entrance relatively small in comparison to the main building. The entrance is located right next to the main mass. From year to year, the museum is constantly used as an exhibition space for many artists.

Via Via Café Yogyakarta
Jalan Prawirotaman 30
Yogyakarta, Central Java 55153
Eko Prawoto
1995

069 B

Via Via Café is located in a crowded area known as the tourist district of Yogyakarta. The café is a member of the Livingstone Group, a non-profit tourism organisation. Via Via Café is deliberately designed to be a meeting point for travellers from all over the world. The café is also available in Europe, South America, Africa and Asia in cities such as Leuven, Copan, Agacucho, Buenos Aires, Dakar, Mopti, Arusha, Zanzibar, Antwerpen and Kathmandu. In keeping with Livingstone's mission, Via Via Café is driven by the aim to facilitate sustainable tourism. In such a location, the traveller is expected to meet other fellow travellers and local communities for cultural exchange and a sharing of experiences. The local architect chosen for this project, EkoPrawoto, rediscovers the four visions of a meeting point: openness, equality, communication, and wonderment. The architect then interpreted these visions into a two-storey building with a façade dominated by bamboo with a fibre roof. Since its opening, Via Via Café has successfully become the meeting point for local and international tourists.

Cemeti Art House
Jalan D.I. Panjaitan No. 41
Yogyakarta, Central Java 55143
Eko Prawoto
1998

070 B

Cemeti Art House is one of the most active contemporary art galleries in Yogyakarta. The building, a combination of traditional Javanese architecture and contemporary architecture, is the result of the collaboration between architect Eko Prawoto and the owners of the gallery, the artists Mella Jarsma and Nindityo. Within this gallery are areas that are open, closed, high-ceilinged, and low-ceilinged to accommodate the various needs of each artist. Elements of old and modern architecture are combined to depict the dynamics of the well-established art scene of Yogyakarta. At the front of the building, guests are welcomed by a joglo-style pavilion taken from Kasongan Village. This pavilion is dominated by bamboo and wooden tables, chairs, and doors to enhance the impression of antiqueness in the gallery. Further inside, beginning from the corridor, the interior is predominantly constructed with concrete walls painted in plain colours without any ornamentation, enhancing the modern impression of the gallery.

Greenhost Boutique Hotel

Jalan Prawirotaman II No. 629
Brontokusuman, Yogyakarta
Central Java 55153
tim tiga
2013

071 B

Greenhost Boutique Hotel is constructed on a 1,700 m² area. During its planning stage, the Spirit of Place concept – the idea that each location has its own characteristics – was given special consideration. Once the characteristics of the location were determined, Paulus Mintarga merged the hotel with the creative activities in the Prawirotaman area and Indonesian agriculture. More than merely a place to stay, the ninety-six-room hotel combines land cultivation as well as arts and crafts in a number of unique and creative facilities, such as an art kitchen, tea spa, Genetika concept store, as well as a creative sharing space, and Greenhost City Farm on the rooftop. The hotel was built using reused materials, such as waste wood, and rejected materials such as CNP iron profile. Today Greenhost Hotel also facilitates educative and creative activities, evidenced in an arts and crafts exhibition on the ground floor and training sessions held by hydroponic farming communities.

Nasirun Gallery
Jalan Wates KM 3, Bantul
Yogyakarta, Central Java 55182
Eko Prawoto
2010

072 B

Nasirun, a famous Yogyakarta-based sculptor, turned a plot of land inside the Bayeman Permai housing complex into an art space, complete with a private studio, museum, and garden. In the garden is a pandanus plant taken from Pangandaran Beach after a tsunami, a living *monument* in memory of the disaster. The gallery is also home to rare artworks created by famous Indonesian artists, such as Basuki Abdullah, Otojaya, and Fadjar Sidik, as well as being a historical record for the passage of Indonesian arts from era to era. Nasirun Gallery was designed by Eko Prawoto. The unique feature of this structure is the sequential ramps circling the building that lead to the second-floor exhibition gallery. The ramps were designed so as to each offer a different spatial experience: one is located next to the fish pond; another is made of used railroad ties; the floor of another is covered in black stone with its roof a painted skylight, and finally there is a ramp covered by a bamboo canopy.

Ngibikan Village Reconstruction

RT 05/RW 14, Dusun Ngibikan
Bantul, Yogyakarta
Central Java 55781
Society of Ngibikan Village
2006

This village was utterly destroyed by the tectonic earthquake of Yogyakarta on 27 May 2006. While most of the earthquake victims were living in tents, the Society of Ngibikan Village had started to think of reconstructing their village. Supervised by architect Eko Prawoto, the society reused salvaged materials combined with coconut timber to construct the frame of their houses. The frames were a transformation of the traditional limasan house measuring 6 m² x 7.2 m². The partitions in the interior of the houses were added and designed according to the needs of each family. The process of reconstructing the village was based on the principle of *mutual assistance*. In just ninety days sixty-five houses were built. As time passes by, the creativity of each villager in applying their own personal touch to their respective house is visible, giving birth to a new identity. The reconstruction of the village was shortlisted for the 2010 Aga Khan Award for Architecture.

Bumi Pemuda Rahayu

Munthuk Village, Dlingo District
Yogyakarta, Central Java 55783
Effan Adhiwira, Marco Kusumawijaya, Yuli Kusworo
2012

074 B

Rujak Centre for Urban Studies, led by Marco Kusumawijaya, initiated Bumi Pemuda Rahayu (BPR) – a place for multi-disciplinary workshop activities, located close to the South Square of Yogyakarta. The construction process also involved Arkom (Arsitek Komunitas, or Community Architects), a group of young architects who provide architectural services for marginalised groups, indigenous villages, environmental and cultural preservations, as well as disaster response activities. Arkom's founder, Yuli Kusworo, led the construction of the large hall together with the community and local residents mostly skilled in carpentry. The collaboration was intended to create a facility that would be continuously used by the locals in a sustainable manner. The collaboration also involved Andesh Tomo and a bamboo expert, Effan Adhiwira, to practise the skill of bamboo processing. This opportunity was eventually used as a means to increase the knowledge of the surrounding communities.

The open multifunctional hall, known by locals as *Rumah Bambu* – or Bamboo House – was built in collaboration with locals, architects and bamboo experts

Sendangsono Pilgrimage Complex

Desa Banjaroyo, Kalibawang
Kulon Progo, Yogyakarta
Central Java 55672
Y. B. Mangunwijaya
1974

Sendangsono is a Catholic pilgrimage complex whose surroundings were designed by the humanist and clergyman Y. B. Mangunwijaya. Volcanic stone is the dominant material applied to the areas within this serene complex. In 1991, Sendangsono was awarded the Ikatan Arsitek Indonesia Award in the Special Building category.

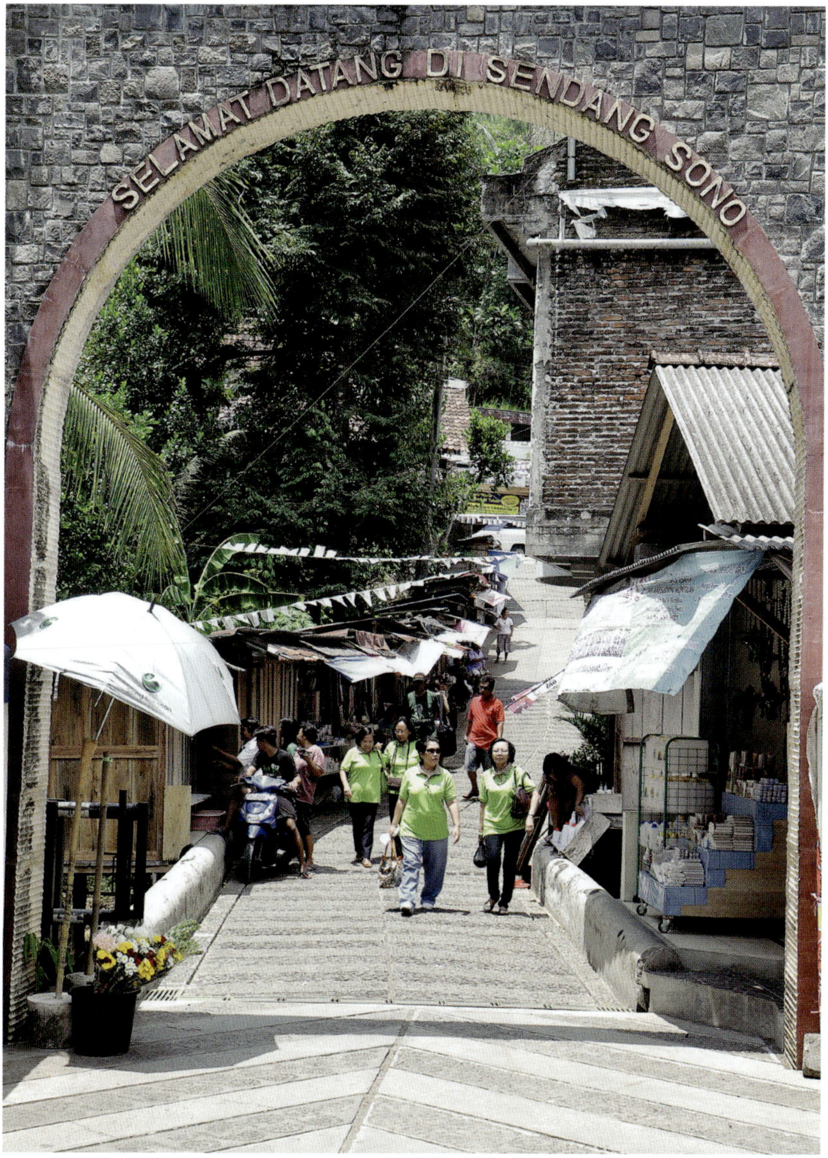
SELAMAT DATANG DI SENDANG SONO

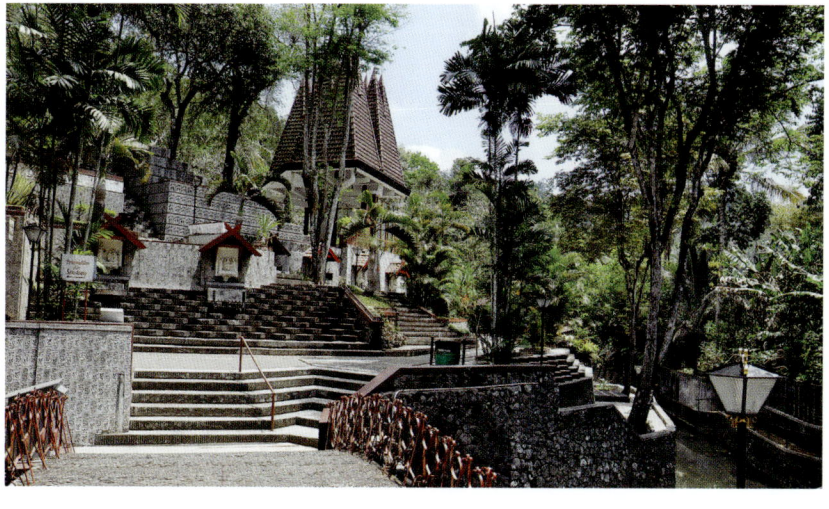

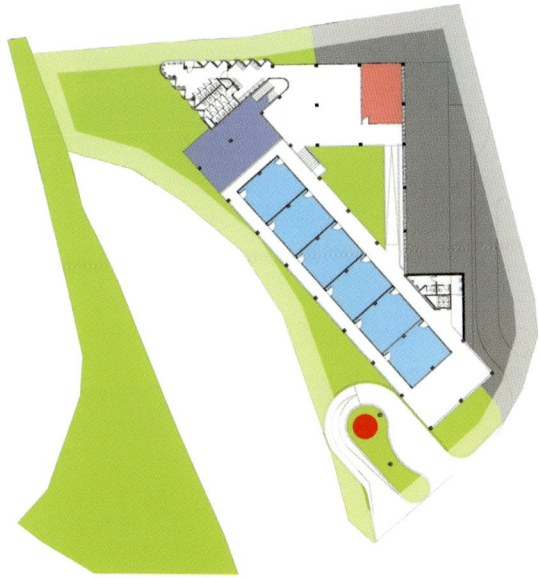

Maria Regina School
Palm Hill Estate
Jalan Palm Hill 2 No. 1
Semarang, Central Java 50232
Adi Purnomo
2008

The school building, made of exposed concrete, is situated on a steep triangular site inside a housing complex in North Semarang. The architect responded to the area that covers 3,000 m² with a four-storey-high vertical development that accommodates classes from preschool to junior high. The kindergarten is placed on the ground floor, while the primary school and junior high school are on the upper floors, with consideration given to facilitating evacuation in the event of disaster. The classes are located on the outer sides of the site, leaving a triangular open area in the middle of the building. Ramps, deemed safer and more enjoyable for students, are used to connect the floors. Since the building is exposed to a fair amount of sunlight, concrete fins have been applied to provide shade for the classrooms. Additionally, perforated metal panels are also applied as a source of shade for several parts of the building.

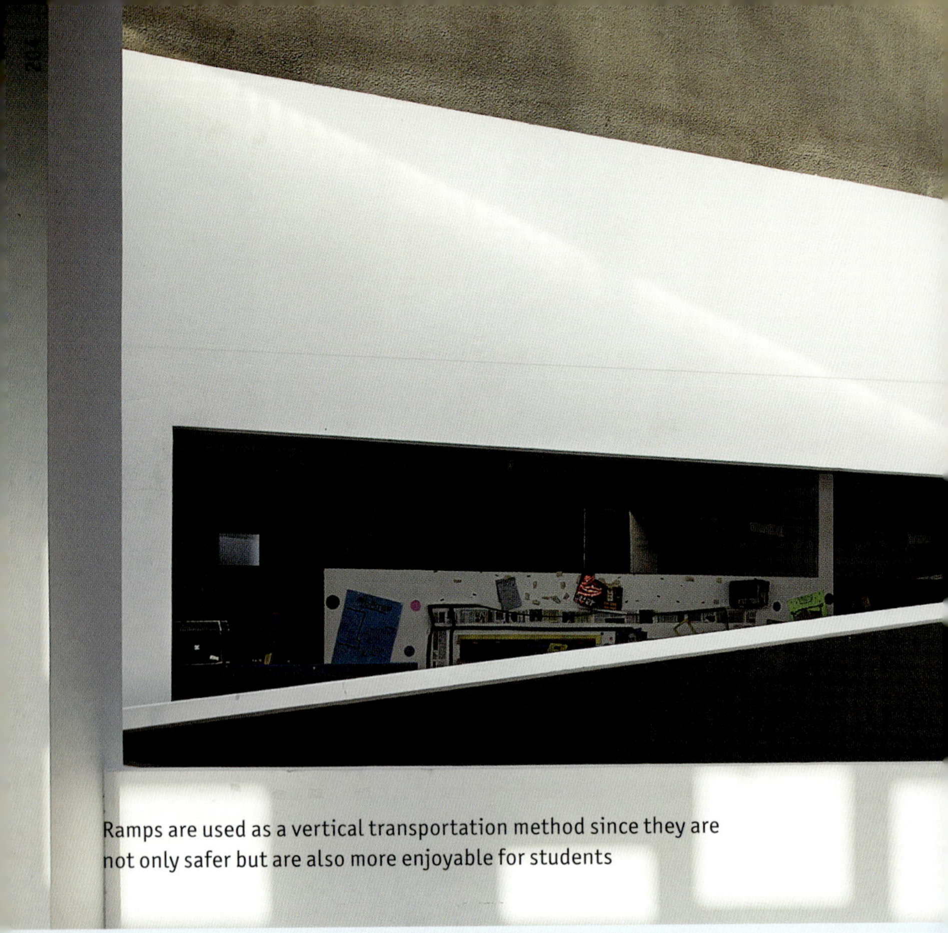

Ramps are used as a vertical transportation method since they are not only safer but are also more enjoyable for students

Concrete fins are a response to the prevailing amount of sunlight, providing shade for classrooms

Rempah Rumah Karya

Tegalmulyo RT02 RW04, Gajahan
Colomadu, Surakarta
Central Java 57135
tim tiga
2010

The construction of Rempah Rumah Karya was motivated by the need to remove the scraps of the construction of the old warehouse whose contract had expired. As they were removed, it became apparent that these scraps were reusable, and so they were adopted as the materials for the construction of Rempah Rumah Karya. Some of the construction scraps are used as CNP steel profiles arranged in closed curves, forming the main frames of the building. The outer walls are made from steel frames with wooden and glass panels attached to them; the garden lamps from used PVC pipes; the interior decoration from car licence plates, and so on. In the end, Rempah Rumah Karya is more than merely a warehouse, but also constitutes an active workshop that openly accommodates creative arts and cultural activities, from exhibitions and community meetings, to creative works for students at elementary school.

Rumah Turi
Jalan Srigading II No. 12
Solo, Central Java 57139
tim tiga
2008

078 B

Rumah Turi is an eco-boutique resort that connects its guests to nature, communities, arts, culture, and – more importantly – other guests. A minimum investment producing a maximum result was the main idea behind the design, achieved through the implementation of sustainable building ideas and thus creating a building that saves energy and is cost-efficient.

The success of the implementation of this concept led the building to be selected as the Best Tropical Building as part of the ASEAN Energy Awards 2012. One feature of the sustainable building concept implemented in the resort is the urban farming idea, illustrated by the vertical garden and vegetable patch on the upper floor. Reusing waste wood for both furniture and the parquet floor is also part of the sustainable building concept. To save water, waste water and rain water are naturally filtered by vetiver grass and then reused for watering plants or flushing toilets.

Bank Indonesia Solo
Jalan Jenderal Sudirman No. 4
Solo, Central Java 57133
Eduard Cuypers. Conservation:
Han Awal and Partners
2012

Initially, the building was used as the representative office of Bank Indonesia in Solo. It was built over the course of two years, 1908–1910, by the Dutch architects E. Cuypers, M.J. Hulswit, and G.H. Fermont. The Indonesian architect H. Awal, the founder of Han Awal & Partners, was assigned by Bank Indonesia Solo to restore the heritage building. The architect demolished additional structures and renovated damaged parts, restoring the building to its original shape. In the future, the building will be turned into a museum.

Bank Indonesia Solo (Extension)

Jalan Jenderal Sudirman No. 4
Solo, Central Java 57133
Han Awal
2012

080 B

The new building of Bank Indonesia (BI) Solo was constructed as a response to the need for increasing office spaces. To meet demand, in 2010 a competition for the design of the BI Solo extension was held. Bank Indonesia outlined two specific requirements: first, the new building had to be able to represent the gracefulness of the old Bank Indonesia Solo building located right next to it, a condition termed *harmony by contrast*, and secondly, the building had to appear modern without seeming at odds with local Javanese culture. Architect Han Awal won the design competition. The design approach that he adopted involved directing the orientation of the new building mass towards the two most important axes of Solo. First, the block of the building mass that faces Jalan Sudirman was directed towards the Vastenberg Fort-Pasar Gede axis. The building mass itself was withdrawn into the back of the site, symbolising the philosophy of Javanese architecture. Secondly, the main building mass was directed towards Vastenberg Fort, Puro Mangkunegaran and Keraton Hadiningrat. A bridge that crosses over Jalan Ronggowarsito was constructed to connect the old and new buildings of Bank Indonesia Solo.

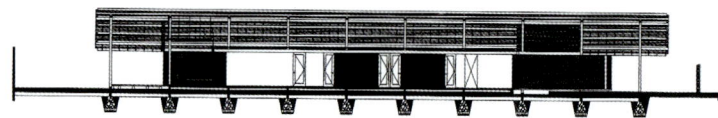

Javaplant

Jalan Raya Solo Tawangmangu
KM 82 No. 33, Central Java
Solo 57712
andramatin
2000

Javaplant is an office building designed for a client who makes his business by manufacturing traditional medicines known as *jamu*. The client wanted an office for his company's herbal extract factory, since his long-standing activity in the export and import sector means that the company is often visited by guests from abroad, requiring an impressive representative office. The site of this office is located on a mountainous area. Architect Andra Matin actually felt compelled to preserve the simplicity of the surrounding nature; nature is thus thought of as supporting the architecture. In contrast to the client's wish, the architect avoided a majestic, luxurious, and hi-tech building. Javaplant was eventually designed as a single-storey building with a stretch of linear configuration underneath a saddle roof. Seen from the outside, the building appears to blend with the horizon. The building won the 2006 IAI DKI Award.

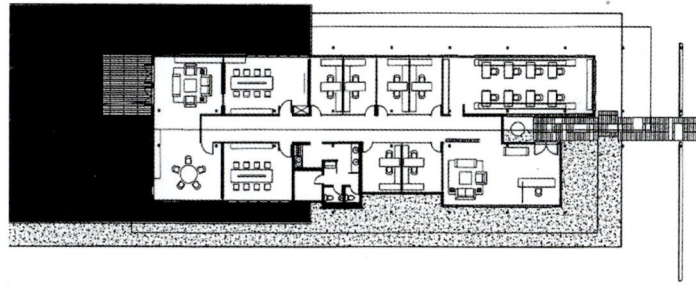

Santa Maria Assumpta Church 082 B
Jalan Andalas No. 24, Klaten
Central Java 57413
Y. B. Mangunwijaya
1968

The Santa Maria Assumpta church was inaugurated on 8 December 1968 by Bishop Julius Kardinal Darmajuwana. Its name was changed from Beata Virgo a Sacratissimo Sacramento to the Parish of Santa Maria Assumpta Klaten. Later on, the church would become known for its ability to accentuate simplicity, familiarity, and openness. Just like other churches designed by Y.B. Mangunwijaya (affectionately known as Romo Mangun), the church was built with a clean and humble shape. The floor plan is a simple square without walls and is covered by a limasan roof, much like the shape of the *pendopo*, the traditional pavilion that cannot be separated from Javanese culture. The richness of shape and meaning found in any of Romo Mangun's works can also be clearly discerned in the church, namely in the application of Javanese cultural elements such as *pendapa, siti hinggil, soko guru,* and *pringgitan*. The shape of the church itself is often thought to resemble a bird spreading its wings, with some interpreting the relief on the outer wall as the symbol of the tree of life.

Open Museum of Trowulan Archaeological Site

Jalan Pendo Agung, Trowulan
Mojokerto, East Java 61374
Y. B. Mangunwijaya
1968

083 B

The design for this open museum began with a design competition for the master plan and open museum in the Pusat Informasi Majapahit (PIM, or Majapahit Information Centre) area, arranged by the evaluation team of PIM Trowuland and the Indonesian Institute of Architects (IAI). The competition was held for a full month and was won by a collaboration between Han Awal & Partners Architects and Mamostudio in 2010. The Open Museum of Trowulan Archaeological Site stands on a conservation site in the Museum of Trowulan area, where the latest remnants of Majapahit were found. The initial idea was to create a structure with minimum contact to the ground, but without requiring the use of heavy equipment during the construction process. It is also expected to shelter as much of the excavation site as possible. The main structure of this open museum consists of modular frames shaped as inverted pyramids. Bamboo, wood, steel, glass, and other materials are used as needed, based on the level of permanency of the construction and the available budget.

Soekarno Memorial Park
Jalan Kalasan No. 1, Blitar
East Java 66133
Baskoro Tedjo
2008

Initially, the municipal government of Blitar requested architect Baskoro Tedjo to design a public library in the vicinity. However, based on his research, the architect concluded that a conventional library would not attract public interest. Eventually, through cross-programming, the architect attempted to utilise the area around the burial place of Ir. Soekarno. He thus designed a library in the area to attract tourists and the Soekarno Memorial Place was born. The library itself was designed to be integrated with existing functions. The architect then created a new axis which led to the grave of Bung Karno (the nickname of Ir. Soekarno) by directing visitors to pass through the library area. On the other hand, the grave was determined as the tip of the axis; therefore the height of the library building was not allowed to exceed the height of the roof over the grave. Adopting the roof of nearby Candi Panataran, the library is also covered by a flat roof.

Hotel Tugu
Jalan Tugu No. 3, Malang
East Java 65119
Duta Cermat Mandiri
1990

085 B

Malang, a city once dubbed the most beautiful in Southeast Asia during the Dutch colonial era, is well known for its excellent urban planning, apple orchards, and tea plantations – and Hotel Tugu is located right at the heart of it. Hotel Tugu is situated at the Alun-Alun Bunder, or Malang Plaza. In response to the town hall, municipal building and round plaza, the hotel's façade is designed as a curve. In general, the architecture of Hotel Tugu follows the style of colonial architecture. Hotel Tugu was the first hotel designed by Budiman Hendropurnomo, the principal architect of the DCM architectural firm. DCM designed the exterior of Hotel Tugu in an eclectic fashion, representing an amalgamation of several architectural styles and cultures. As a counterbalance, the interior of the hotel is designed neutrally to allow the owner of the hotel to exhibit his artwork collection here. The most famous artwork in the hotel is the portrait of a long-haired woman named Oei Hui-lan, the daughter of a sugar magnate and the wife of V. K. Wellington Koo, the Chinese ambassador to France, Great Britain and the United States in the 1930s and 1940s. The building won the 1991 IAI National Award. Hotel Tugu is a two-and-a-half-hour's drive from Surabaya.

Intiland Tower Surabaya

Jalan Panglima Sudirman
Surabaya, East Java 60271
Paul Rudolph
1997

It is not hard to find Intiland Tower in Surabaya. The building is a rented office space consisting of twelve floors with two basements. Seen from its side, the composition of this white tower consists of several isosceles triangles whose sharp angles face upwards with masses of parallelograms in between them. On each floor of each building mass are eaves with different orientations. The eaves on the triangular masses are tilted to the back, while the parallelograms' eaves are tilted to the front. The eaves' angle follows the angle of the building mass on which they are located. These eaves not only shield the interior of the building from glaring sunlight, but also create shade and reduce the temperature of the microclimate in the building. Paul Rudolph, an American architect, adopted this design approach based on tropical architecture known as *roof architecture*. This can also be seen in the Wisma Dharmala building in Jakarta, also designed by Rudolph.

De Soematra
Jalan Sumatera No. 75
Surabaya, East Java 60281
Hidayat Endramukti
1910

087 B

De Soematra is a multifunctional boutique hotel that occupies a heritage building. This was built by the Dutch in 1910. Initially, the building was used by AIA (Algemeen Ingenieurs en Architecten Bureau), a famous architectural firm during the Dutch colonial era. After a change in ownership the building was converted into De Soematra. The name of the hotel has been adjusted to suit the name of the street where the building is located. Several additional architectural elements were inserted into this historical building, although these were created in such a way so as not to alter the original structure. The exterior of the building has been preserved in order to take visitors back to the Dutch colonial era. However, the interior's new design has been implemented in a classic American style by the interior designer Hidayat Endramukti, who created different interior themes for each room. The foyer is dominated by purple; the Indigo Room is dominated by blue; the library is all red, while nuances of the classic American style are easily palpable in the lounge. De Soematra is also equipped with a dining room, bar, backyard terrace and a garden. The colonial garden concept has been adopted for the wide grass lawn. Padma, a landscape architect from La Padma, chose the plants within the garden in accordance with the said colonial garden concept. Colonial gardens are generally formal gardens, and to create this impression, rows of palm trees were planted on the front lawn. On the inner court, the existing large rain tree (*Albizia saman*) – whose diameter reaches 1 m – is preserved as part of the history of the building. The building is now mostly used for high-end events. De Soematra was inaugurated as a cultural heritage building in 2012.

1903 Restaurant

Jalan Sumatera 40, Surabaya
East Java 60281
Hermawan Dasmanto
2013

1903 is a restaurant built in keeping with a classical European style and was restored by architect Hermawan Dasmanto. This fine dining restaurant is located in the Society Complex, Surabaya, right next to the Historica Coffee and Pastry. 1903 occupies a heritage building more than one hundred years old, whose first stone was laid by Sophie E. Scheel on 18 May 1903.

Historica Coffee and Pastry
Jalan Sumatera 40, Surabaya
East Java 60281
Hermawan Dasmanto
2014

089 B

This café is one of the two facilities available in the Society Complex, Surabaya. Besides designing Coffee and Pastry, architect Hermawan Dasmanto also took part in designing the entire interior of the Society Complex, which takes up three historical buildings. For the interior, the architect mostly uses arches to imitate the Empire-style architecture found in the colonial building next to the complex. These arches are applied as ceiling and wall accents.

Interior of Historica Coffee and Pastry

Hotel Majapahit

Jalan Tunjungan No. 65
Surabaya, East Java 60275
L. Martin Sarkies.
Redesigned by: C. P. Wolff Sc
1910

090 B

Hotel Majapahit was built during the Dutch colonial era by L. Martin Sarkies. At the time the hotel was known as Hotel Oranje. The hotel's opening ceremony was attended by Princess Astrid of Sweden, Charlie Chapman, and the Crown Prince Leopold III of Belgium. In 1930, Wolff Schoemaker, a Dutch architect, redesigned the hotel by adding touches of art déco to the façade. During the Japanese occupation, the hotel was renamed Hotel Yamato. The hotel is also famous as the place where *the Hotel Yamato Incident*, a milestone in the history of Indonesia's independence, took place.

Musholla Kompleks Banyuwangi

Jalan Sritanjung, Banyuwangi
East Java 68414
andramatin
2014

091 B

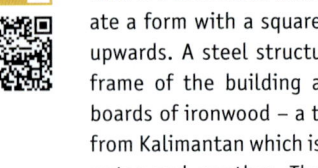

The small musholla is located within the official residence complex of the Regent of Banyuwangi in East Java. The musholla is an extension of the old musholla building which became insufficient. Architect Andra Matin did not expand the old building, but rather created a new building right next to it with a completely different design. The basic premise of the new building's form is a cube *sliced* in several parts to create a form with a square base that tapers upwards. A steel structure is used as the frame of the building and is covered in boards of ironwood – a type of hard wood from Kalimantan which is resistant to both water and weather. The building is surrounded by water to direct the circulation to one side, as well as making the building appear to float on water. The area reserved for ablutions is covered with a grassy slope and stone wall so that it appears sunken underground. Ultimately, the building looks more like a piece of art or a sculpture that should adorn a garden. And that is exactly what the architect wanted.

A closer look at the musholla from the inside and outside

Blimbingsari Airport ⌃⌄
Bayuwangi, East Java 66133
andramatin
2015 in stages

092 B

Its construction commencing in 2013, the airport is designed so as to appear to burst with tropical architectural nuances. It features wide eaves, a cross-ventilation system, a skylight, and also wooden boards for walls. In some areas these wooden boards are closely arranged so as to obstruct any outside view, but they are also openly arranged in other places to provide one. The gaps between the boards also act as circulation channels for sea air, given that the airport is located on the coast of the easternmost part of Java. The architect deliberately averts the futuristic image of most airports and opts to enhance its local features. Traditional architecture belonging to the Osing – the indigenous tribe of Banyuwangi descended from the people of the Majapahit Empire – appears in the design in the form of the modified roof, which is designed so as to be covered in grass. Banyuwangi's plentiful resources are also represented by using local materials as much as possible.

Pendopo Bupati Banyuwangi »
Jalan Sritanjung, Banyuwangi
East Java 68414
Adi Purnomo
2012

093 B

In Javanese, *pendopo* means *pillared pavilion*. In this context, pendopo is the official residence of the Regent of Banyuwangi,

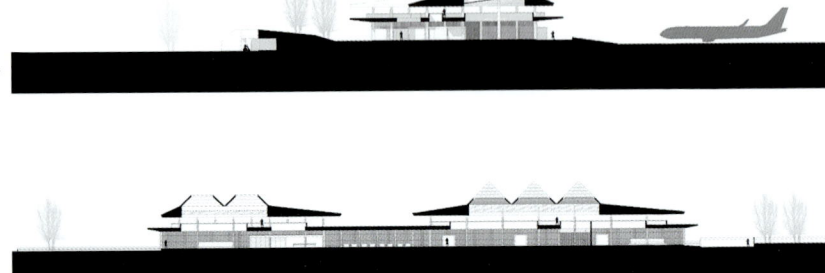

as well as an area that functions as a gathering hall where the Regent receives official guests: a pavilion-like structure built on columns with no walls. At the time of renovation, the building was practically abandoned and deformed. Adi Purnomo renovated this particular building by restoring its original shape as much as possible. As a means to demonstrate this, he rebuilt the back porch, a distinctive characteristic of Indische architecture, which was previously closed and used as a kitchen. This was not an easy thing to do because of the lack of documentation of historical buildings in Indonesia, and due to the fact that original materials used in its construction are no longer available. To give a breath of fresh air, several details are adapted to current conditions.

Guest House Banyuwangi
Jalan Sritanjung, Banyuwangi
East Java 68414
Adi Purnomo
2012

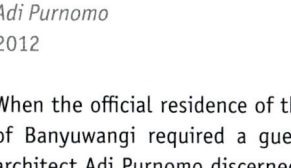

When the official residence of the Regent of Banyuwangi required a guest house, architect Adi Purnomo discerned that the official residence complex was a Dutch heritage compound with unique European architecture. He did not wish to intrude upon the uniqueness of the architecture, but at the same time did not wish to create a duplicate of the colonial building. Therefore, the architect decided to build the guest house on one side of the site: a gently sloping area covered in grass with natural stone walls. This method made the guest house appear as a feature of a garden buried underground. On the other hand, the presence of the historical building becomes more pronounced among the green gardens. The interesting feature of this clever method is the emergence of *chimneys* among the green grass which are actually skylights and ventilations for the *underground* rooms. Each room has an open area facing towards the side of the site, so that guests do not feel as confined as the façade suggests. This clever method presents a good example of how to design a new building within a historical building complex.

To emphasise the presence of the historical building, the guest house was buried underground and forms a feature of the garden

Bali

Island of the Gods is commonly used as an epithet for this majestic island

Widely known as one of the most beautiful islands in the world with breathtaking beaches, Bali never fails to attract tourists from all over the world

Bali and Architecture for Tourism

Imelda Akmal

The architecture of Bali cannot be separated from its tourism. Bali is a relatively small island in Indonesia that is well known all over the world. In fact, it is even more famous than the large country in which it is located. This is because the island is one of the most sought-after tourism destinations in the whole world, even though its total land area comprises only about 0.3 per cent of the whole area of Indonesia.

Bali's fame does not stem merely from its colourful and gentle beaches, or its terraced rice fields which seem as if they were carved by gods, or even its unique and singular culture and traditional ceremonies, but also because the Dutch systematically promoted Bali to the world during their colonial reign in Indonesia. According to Michel Picard, author of, amongst others, *Bali: tourisme culturel et culture touristique* (Paris: L'Harmattan,

1992), the last three kingdoms in Bali, Tabanan, Badung, and Klungkung were not conquered through war, but through *puputan*, in which the king and his *ksatria* (knights) went to battlefield wearing their best clothes and adornments and committed suicide or murdered their own friends. They also hurled their gold accoutrements towards the Dutch soldiers as an insult to the Dutch colonial government who wished to conquer the severely disadvantaged Balinese kingdoms by brute force. This made the Dutch colonial government abashed, and to hide this, they bestowed Bali with privileges, such as allowing them to keep their Hindu faith and traditions, and prohibiting the entry of other religions (especially Islam and Christianity). Soon after, the Dutch launched a massive tourism promotion for Bali, especially at the World Tourism Exhibition in France in 1931, to attract European tourists. These European tourists were amazed by the beauty of the natural landscape of Bali: its beaches, rice fields, lakes, and volcanoes. The strange and fascinating traditional ceremonies became unparalleled spectacles, and the beauty of Balinese people became the talk of the century. All of these mesmerising features attracted many visitors from the West, including painters, poets, photographers, researchers, and writers who produced novels, travelogues, and so on. Numerous epithets were given to Bali, including *The Last Paradise*.

Sanur Beach, a famous area since the earliest tourist development in Bali

Following the growth of tourism, a number of facilities were built – especially places to stay. When the Dutch pulled out of Indonesia and President Sukarno (also a descendant of Bali) served as the head of the country, he also treated Bali as a special place. On this small island a large, magnificent and massive hotel was built during this particular era with funds taken from the war damage compensation and restitution from Japan. This hotel was part of the Nation Building projects, and one of Sukarno's *lighthouse projects*. It was named the Bali Beach Hotel and was designed by Taisei Construction from Japan. Bali Beach Hotel was also the tallest building outside Jakarta at that time (and still to this day is the tallest building in Bali). The imposing edifice agitated the Balinese so much that after the hotel was built a regulation stipulating that the height of any building in Bali should not exceed the height of a coconut tree was passed.

Despite this regulation, the development of tourism facilities in Bali marched on. Indonesia's second President, Soeharto, opened a new area, covering 425 ha south of the airport, which he named Nusa Dua. Foreign architects were assigned to design five-star hotels with thousands of rooms and a convention centre. Some names include PTW Architects, who designed the Nusa Dua Beach Hotel,

A rich and fertile landscape can be found in most parts of Bali Island

Emilio Nadal, who designed Mélia Bali Sol Hotel, and Marc Hertrich, architect of the Club Méditerranée hotel: Nusa Dua was geared up for international conventions. The architecture of the hotels in Bali is evidently aimed at foreign guests who wish to enjoy the natural tropical climate while indulging in world-class luxuries. This is evident in the hotels' spatial programmes and completeness of their amenities. As for the appearance of the hotels, it is usually illustrated by the amalgamation of Balinese architecture and current building technology. Besides these giant hotels, villas and/or boutique hotels are also emerging. Bali was so frenzied with foreign guests at one point that the island was the only province not to suffer from the economic crisis that severely hit Indonesia between 1998 and 2000. Bali even boldly used US dollars for business transactions in order to reap even bigger profits, thus becoming too expensive for local tourists.

Then, a shocking incident happened in the early 2000s. Tourism in Bali was forced to stand still when a couple of bombs exploded in the years 2002 and 2005. These suicide bombings constituted a profound trauma for the families, friends, and countries of the victims (mostly Australians). Travel warnings were consequently issued from a number of countries: Bali was crippled.

Some people whose livelihood depended on tourism suffered heavily, as did art performances which were usually held to entertain guests. During this dark time, Bali – which had been accustomed to enjoying the windfalls from foreign guests – collapsed, at least for two long years. And so, Bali began to take a gander at local tourists.

Fortunately, just after 2005, Indonesians were finally free from the shackles of economic crisis, and a new wave of middle-class citizens who had just discovered the joys of travelling emerged. Local investors began to invest in the construction of tourism facilities aimed at local tourists, especially budget hotels. The behaviour of local tourists is of course vastly different from that of foreign tourists. Hours of sunbathing mean little to them considering that the sun shines over Indonesia all year round. Thus, for them, hotels need not be located by the seaside. Local first-time travellers generally choose economical hotels with air conditioned rooms. They arrive in droves with their extended families, and are fond of shopping and culinary tours. Therefore, in addition to hotels, malls and restaurants are also growing rapidly to meet this particular demand. Cheap hotels grow like mushrooms in the rainy season, especially on the southern side of the island, near Tuban Airport. In this climate, Indonesian architects gained the opportunity to design hotels designated for these recent waves of tourists. For instance, Antony Liu and Ferry Ridwan of Studio Tonton

Not only its beaches, but also its paddy rice fields and mountains attract tourists to Bali

are some of the architects whose many designs can be found in Bali. The Bale, a boutique hotel in Nusa Dua, is one of the designs by Studio TonTon that attracted the attention of the architectural world. Budiman Hendropurnomo already had a head start with his design for Maya Ubud Hotel which was succeeded by several other hotels, such as Maya Sanur. Popo Danes and Ketut Arthana are two senior architects from Bali who have been most productive in designing various hotels, villas, and resorts – both public and private – in the land of their birth. They are also two of the most highly regarded architects in Indonesia. Today, their footsteps are followed by young Balinese architects such as Putu Edy Semara (ESA Architect), Jeghier, Cok Gung Pramanayogi, and others.

Nowadays, tourism facilities in Bali are all-inclusive for local and foreign tourists, from economical facilities to super luxurious resorts. Bali Island is also one of the regions in Indonesia with the most aggressive construction activities. This aggressive development certainly has its own negative impacts, one of which is Bali's uncontrollable population density. Architect Gede Kresna, who preferred to practise architecture in the village where he was born, once said, »Learn not from the successes of Bali's tourism, but from its failures.« However, Bali is still an interesting destination for architectural tourism. With more than four thousand accommodations listed on hotel booking websites, there is no place as rich as Bali when it comes to references for architectural tourism.

Bali is also renowned as a place to enjoy spectacular sunsets.

C

Coconut trees are commonly found along the pavements in Bali

Gunung Agung, Bali's tallest and most sacred mountain, is known as home to the Hindu gods and a dwelling place for ancestral spirits

Hinduism is an inseparable part of living in Bali

Bali's unique Hinduism culture is particularly famous for its rich and vibrant arts

Art is a part of everyday life for Balinese people

In Bali, artwork – such as statues – is a part of religion which can easily be found at any corner or junction

Tourism has profoundly changed Bali's environment

Tourist facilities, such as hotels and villas, have been built expansively across the rice fields

Sawahs (rice fields) are a favourite tourist attraction which have driven businesses to develop accommodation in the middle of rice fields

Gunung Agung, Bali's tallest and most iconic volcanic mountain, acts as a mecca for Bali Hinduism: traditionally, all houses and temples face this mountain.

C

Conrad Wedding Chapel
Jalan Pratama 168
Nusa Dua 80363
Studio TonTon & andramatin
2006

095 C

The iconic-shaped chapel is located on the shores of Tanjung Benoa in the Nusa Dua tourism complex. The combination of ideas from two famous architectural firms, Studio TonTon and andramatin, resulted in the asymmetrical triangular chapel. The shape of the building mass represents the relations of God, men, and nature. The asymmetric design is apparent in the contrast of materials that represent the masculine – the solid mass from travertine – and the feminine – the transparent mass made of glass – aspects of humanity. The chapel is built floating on a reflecting pool with a long pathway serving as the main access. Rows of lamps are placed along the single main access to light the way to the chapel at night. Within the chapel, the view across the wide open sea and sky is the main vista. Conrad Wedding Chapel is able to hold three hundred people and is one of the most preferred wedding venues in Indonesia. Studio TonTon was awarded the 2006 IAI Jakarta award for this project.

Amarterra Villas

BTDC Resort Lot Block B
Nusa Dua 80363
Wastu Adi Olahrupa
2012

096 C

The Nusa Dua district in southern Bali is designed to be an exclusive tourism area and was built in the 1980s. One of the latest facilities inside the district is the Amarterra Villas complex built in 2010. The Amarterra Villas complex consists of thirty-nine units of villas and other supporting facilities on a 20,000 m² area. The whole complex is strictly regulated by the manager and curator, so that no building is taller than one storey. Inspired by the water gardens of Bali, the architect designed the Amarterra Villas with luxuriant water elements, especially in the reception area where a large pond is divided by a gently sloping ramp. The main gate leading to the villa area is situated atop a wide stairway and is designed to resemble the Candi Bentar – the twin gate-like structures that commonly lead to prominent places such as temples or palaces. This gate is inspired by the Trowulan historical site in East Java. The presence of traditional architectural elements in the design for the tropical landscape creates a very palpable Bali atmosphere.

The main gate leading to the villa complex was designed by taking inspiration from the Trowulan historical site in East Java

The Bale

Jalan Raya Nusa Dua Selatan
Kuta Selatan 80363
Studio TonTon
2002

The Bale is a boutique hotel consisting of twenty-nine pavilions. The hotel is virtually the embryo of boutique hotels in Bali. Unlike similar hotels, local Balinese values are not prominent in The Bale, and the hotel's design is focused more on modern architecture. From the entrance to the pavilions, the building masses are designed in geometric shapes with minimal ornamentation. In response to the site's location (on top of a barren limestone hill), Studio TonTon used sandstone as the finishing material for all building masses. Additionally, the architect also responded to the site's contour by placing the pavilions on different contour levels, so that each pavilion commands an unobstructed view of the sea, even though the hotel has no direct access to the beach. In 2002 the architect of this hotel was awarded a citation from IAI Awards in the Commercial Building category, as well as the Best Small Boutique Hotel award in the same year.

Nusa Dua Tourism Project
Nusa Dua 80363
Bali Tourism Development Corporation (BTDC)
1983

The Nusa Dua tourism project is part of the Bali tourism complex development which was planned in 1976. The complex was designed as an integrated tourism area, equipped with luxury accommodation and other amenities. Nusa Dua, a sparsely populated barren area rich in limestone, was chosen as the location for this complex due to the fact that it is quite far away from other Balinese villages. This was deemed necessary in order to reduce the possibility of *polluting* the villages and culture of Bali from the negative impacts of tourism activities. On the other hand, the Nusa Dua area also possesses pristine white sand beaches. The tourism complex began its operation in 1983, and is easily reached from the Ngurah Rai International Airport. After several more developments made by the Bali Tourism Development Corporation (BTDC), Nusa Dua became one of the most sought-after tourism areas in Bali. The tourism complex holds a number of luxury hotels, a convention centre, a shopping centre, a theatre, an eighteen-hole golf course, a hospital, a clinic, a museum, a tourism college, and a pura.

A	Club Med Bali
B	Centara Grand Nusa Dua Resort & Villas
C	Grand Whiz
D	JW Marriott
E	Bali Nusa Dua Convention Centre
F	Kayu Manis Private Villa
G	Nusa Dua Beach Hotel & Spa Bali
H	The Westin Resort Nusa Dua Bali
I	Balinese Villa
J	The Laguna Luxury Collection Resort Spa
K	Museum Pasifika
L	Melia Bali
M	The Bay Nusa Dua CO
N-O	Grand Hyatt Bali & Spa
P	Innaya Putri Bali
Q	Mercure Bali Nusa Dua
R	Courtyard By Marriot Bali
S	Novotel Nusa Dua Hotel & Residences
T	Ayodya Resort Bali S4
U	The Bale
V	The St. Regis Bali

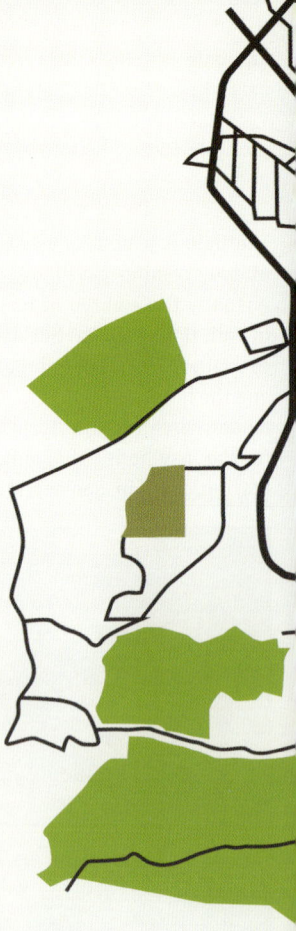

Alila Villas Uluwatu
Jalan Belimbing Sari, Banjar Tambiyak, Desa Pecatu 80364
WOHA
2009

099 C

Alila Villas Uluwatu is located in the barren peninsula. The five-star villa complex was designed by WOHA, an architectural firm based in Singapore. The building masses are divided into one main building and a cluster of villa units. The influence of Majapahit architecture is clearly visible in the massive and volumetric main building which is dominated by natural stone. Not far from the main building is the cantilevered hanging cabana overlooking the Indian Ocean. Unlike the main building's architecture, the cabana was designed with tectonic architecture. The exterior of the cabana is finished with a layer of small wooden slats arranged haphazardly to create a sense of weightlessness. The cabana is also found on each villa unit. Both the one-bedroom and three-bedroom villa units are equipped with a private pool offering a clear view of the horizon.

Potato Head Beach Club Restaurant

Jalan Raya Petitenget
Seminyak 83061
andramatin
2010

Architect Andra Matin, the principal architect and founder of andramatin, designed the Potato Head Beach Club (PHBC), a beach club located on the main road of Seminyak, Bali. Matin designed and developed the PHBC by adopting the concept of *providing attraction*. Seen from afar, the beach club is overwhelming in its gigantic scale. About six thousand mismatched teak window shutters from across the Indonesian archipelago are arranged to form a mosaic that covers the whole 2,500 m² surface area of the building. Behind this mosaic façade, a circular and ascending circulation leads to the interior. The *attraction* concept is also evident in the circular shape of the layout. This circle is cut on one side to provide visual access to the sea – the main attraction and orientation of PHBC. The circular layout is also *stretched* a little bit, creating a somewhat elliptical composition resembling a horseshoe. This also creates an outdoor beach club area at the centre of the circle, forming a spectacular beachfront amphitheatre encircled by two levels of restaurants and bars which overlook the palm tree-fringed beach and Indian Ocean beyond.

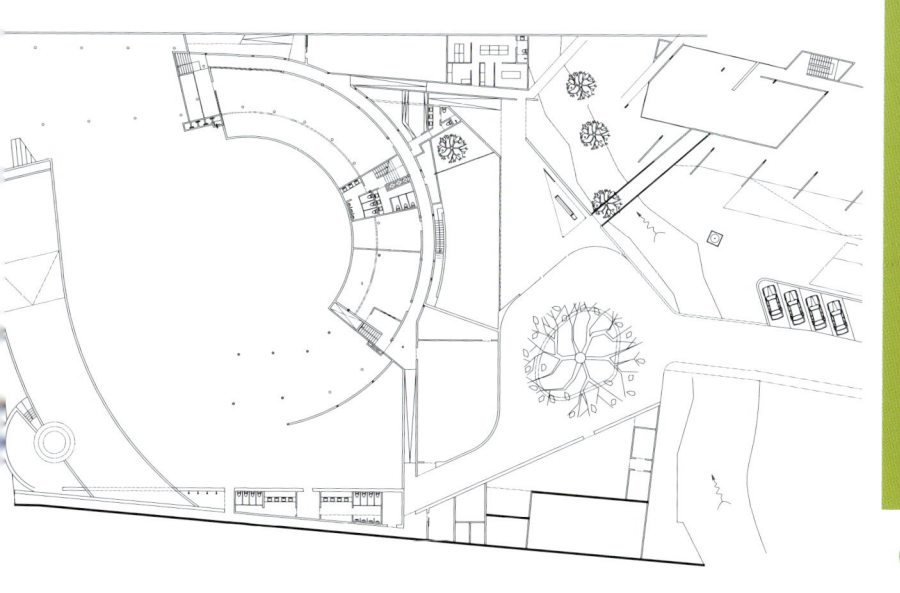

C

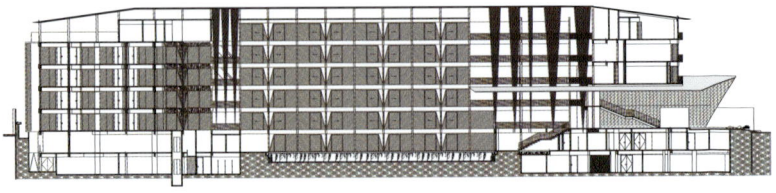

Ize Hotel

Jalan Kayu Aya No. 68
Seminyak 80361
Studio TonTon
2012

Ize Hotel stands on a 1,800 m² area in Seminyak, north of Kuta Beach, in the midst of the uproar caused by the bustle of shops and blaring music from the clubs and cafés. The high air temperature and raucous atmosphere became inevitable problems and so Studio TonTon attempted to combat this by designing a hotel with a cool atmosphere. For public areas such as corridors and the lobby, a porous building cladding was chosen as the main solution for the problems faced by this five-storey hotel. GRC fins measuring 60 cm have been attached to galvanised steel frames to filter the heat of the sun, without obstructing the air flowing between the interior and exterior. These also create interesting and constantly changing shades, following the movement of the sun. Colour play is another solution that creates a sense of coolness in the hotel. Light blue, the colour often associated with the coldness of ice, is chosen as a distinguishing feature amongst the greyness of the hotel walls.

A unique spatial experience is offered at the hotel pool area

Villa Alopa

Jalan Camplung Tanduk
Gang Mangga, Seminyak 80361
SHL Asia
2014

102 C

Villa Alopa, which was designed by SHL Asia, is located in the heart of Seminyak, Bali. The villa is a two-storey building standing on a 350 m² area. The ground floor is reserved for public areas, such as a living room, dining room, and kitchen. Most of the rooms on this floor all open on to the garden and pool area. The upper floor features three bedrooms – one master bedroom and two guest bedrooms. In front of the bedroom there is a balcony which provides circulation.

Oasis Lagoon Sanur

Jalan Danau Tamblingan
No. 136A, Sanur 80228
Sonny Sutanto Architects
2011

Oasis Lagoon Sanur is one of the finest resorts in the tranquil beach village of Sanur, on the southeastern coast of Bali. The interesting aspect of this hotel is that the pointed ends of the saddle roof are designed as steep slopes that reach the ground. This curious design was meant to evoke the impression of a hill when the roof is covered with vines. The roof spans from the lobby to the restaurant, providing a high ceiling over the covered area to impart a sense of spaciousness. From the lobby, guests can sneak a quick look at the rear area that consists of hotel rooms surrounding the swimming pool.

Sudamala Suites

Jalan Sudamala No. 20
Sanur 80227
E. S. A. International
2011

104 C

Located in Sanur, an area famous for being the exclusive home of foreign artists and writers in the 1960s and 1970s, Sudamala Suites offers accommodation and a gallery on a 6,600 m² site. Art exhibitions and performances are not limited to the gallery, but are also performed in the boutique hotel area which contains thirty-five suites. Putu Edy Semara, director of the Esa International architectural firm, wanted Sanur's architecture to be open to other cultures while maintaining its harmony with a typical Balinese vocabulary. No less than three architectural styles – Balinese, European, and Chinese – are fused into the design for this hotel in response to the challenge of presenting a large open space. This requirement *forced* the architect to design two-storey building masses – a practice rarely found in Balinese architecture – to make these proportional to the whole open space arrangement.

Maya Sanur
Jalan Danau Tamblingan
No. 89 M, Sanur 80228
Duta Cermat Mandiri
2015

Located on the main thoroughfare of Sanur, Maya Sanur was designed by Duta Cermat Mandiri (DCM) who experimented with a new building typology for hotels. The design of Maya Sanur is inspired by the shape of a hill – however, the hill of Maya Sanur is not a natural formation but is rather an artificial one designed to break through the conventional typology of hotel buildings. Standing on a 1.3 ha site, the hotel's façade thus constitutes a manmade hill with gentle slopes that beckon guests to climb over to access the beach, situated some 300 m from the hotel. Underneath the manmade hill are the 104 suites of the hotel. The grassy mound helps lower the interior temperature and shields the suites from excessive sunlight. In between these suites, a 180-m-long swimming pool also has the objective to provide guests with a better sense of relaxation.

Tandjung Sari Hotel ⌄

Jalan Danau Tamblingan No. 41
Sanur, Denpasar 80228
Wija Wawo-Runtu
1962

106 C

Prior to purchasing a plot of land in Tanjung Sari, Wija Wawo-Runtu, an artist and entrepreneur, was requested to oversee the Nusa Dua tourism area. Later on, this parcel of land was developed to form Tandjung Sari Hotel. The hotel began as a wicker house designed by Wija Wawo-Runtu, assisted by several local architects, in 1962. Tandjung Sari Hotel became the first hotel to be built on the southern side of Bali. The structure consists of twenty-eight bungalows arranged in a compound, adopting the traditional concept of Balinese villages. The available bungalows are categorised into nine types: village bungalows; new village bungalows; two-storey bungalows, one garden sea view bungalow; beachfront bungalows; twin bedroom bungalows; one family bungalow, and South Garden bungalows. Each bungalow is designed in a Balinese architecture style with its own distinctive character down to the smallest details, such as the carvings on the windows and doors. Tandjung Sari Hotel – frequently visited by international celebrities (the legendary singer Mick Jagger stayed here) – is also equipped with a complete range of modern facilities. Luxury facilities such as a fine dining restaurant, library, swimming pool, and bar are all available within the premises. For some, Tandjung Sari Bar has left a distinct impression. The bar is a blend of modern luxurious and traditional Balinese architecture thatched with cogon grass, complete with the panorama, the sounds of the ocean and the faint sound of *tingklik* (bamboo gamelan) from a distance.

Popo Danes Studio
Jalan Hayam Wuruk No. 159
Denpasar 80235
Popo Danes Architect
2009

Popo Danes Studio is situated on a 2,400 m² area and is an extension of an old house and gallery built by Popo Danes' father. The architect designed the extension as a building with a linear configuration on one side of the plot, while the rest of the plot is set aside for a green open area. The compound construction consists of three floors which accommodate an architectural studio owned by Popo Danes, a work room, a meeting room, and a dining room. In terms of vertical circulation, the architect designed a ramp that allows comfortable access to the second floor. The roof of this building is utilised as a rooftop terrace with a wooden deck for its floor; a thin membrane acts as temporary covering. Nowadays, the studio is also used as a place to practise yoga and Balinese dance. In the future, Popo Danes hopes that his architectural studio will also be used as the gathering place for creative communities more than once every month.

Alila Villas Soori

Banjar Dukuh, Desa Kelating
Kerambitan, Tabanan 82161
SCDA Architects
2008

Alila Villas Soori is a resort complex located in Tabanan, Bali, about one hour's drive from Ngurah Rai International Airport, and an hour from the sacred Tanah Lot Temple. The resort is unique in that it offers its guests a simultaneous view of Batukaru volcano, terraced paddy fields, and the black sand beach that touches the Indian Ocean. As part of an effort to promote energy-saving concepts, SCDA Architects, the Singaporean architectural firm assigned to design this luxurious resort, created connecting corridors which generate microclimate temperatures lower than their surroundings. Moreover, local stone such as the *paras* (sandstone) of Kelating, the paras of Kerobokan, volcanic stone, Sukabumi stone, and river stone are used as an exterior and interior finishing to reduce the temperature inside the building. The application of wide eaves also provides shade and further reduces the overall temperature of the resort.

Millenium Bridge

Jalan Raya Sibang Kaja
Banjar Saren, Abiansemal
Badung 80352
PT Bamboo Pure
2011

Millenium Bridge is a 23-m-long bridge that connects the facilities within the Green School complex in Bali. The bridge that spans over the Ayung River uses 192 bamboo poles for support, a number which was chosen to represent the 192 countries of the world, since the school is a learning facility that educates children from all corners of the globe. Prior to their usage, these bamboo poles were soaked in boric acid solution to prohibit insect infestations that may have weakened the bamboo poles. Another unique feature of the bridge is that its roof has been designed by transforming the shape of the traditional roof of Minangkabau houses found in West Sumatera. Cogon grass (Imperata cylindrica) is used to thatch the roof of the bridge. The whole structure of the Millenium Bridge was designed and built by PT. Bamboo Pure, led by Elora Hardy. The structure was completed in eight months.

Green School
Jalan Raya Sibang Kaja
Banjar Saren, Abiansemal
Badung 80352
PT Bamboo Pure
2018

Standing on a 20 ha area, the Green School offers a new paradigm and concept of learning close to nature. John and Cynthia Hardy's love for the earth compelled them to build a school complex that was completely different from any of the conventional schools found in Indonesia. Through its unique applicable education system, the school is intended to explore students' physical sensitivity to adapt and be adept in facing anything that may happen in the outside world. The school is arguably the pioneer of the return to bamboo as the material of choice in modern architecture in Indonesia. At the moment, the school buildings are some of the first constructions which have been brave enough to exploit on a large scale the advantages of bamboo as a structural and aesthetic element. In the organically shaped

main building, for instance, 2,500 bamboo poles are used as the main structure that holds the 60 m building span. These bamboo poles support the building and form the spiralling, traditionally constructed thatched roof. In other buildings within the Green School complex – the classrooms, assembly room, faculty housing, café, and office – bamboo is used not only as the main structure, but also for the stairways and furniture. Environmentally friendly concepts are applied by using 100 per cent renewable energy, as seen in the use of the photovoltaic panels, the whirlpool-powered generators, biogas and bamboo sawdust for cooking and water-heating purposes. Rather than concrete or asphalt, stone has also been chosen as a material to create walking paths around the school. Volcanic rock has been chosen to build paths, and gravel to build walkways. Since 2008, shortly after the Green School was built, bamboo became increasingly popular as a means to obtain the environmentally friendly and sustainable architecture label.

Fivelements Puri Ahimsa Healing Centre

Banjar Baturning, Desa Mambal
Abiansemal, Badung 80352
Arte Architect and Associates
2010

Fivelements is situated on a 9,000 m² site with a river flanking its southern border. As a facility for physical and spiritual well-being, Fivelements adopted the Tri Hita Karana concept rooted in Balinese culture that teaches about the harmony between man, God, and nature. This concept is also the foundation for the architect in planning the area and the architecture within. The functions within the area are all oriented towards Mount Agung, which is located north of the site. The architect divided the site into three main areas: Utama, Madya, and Nista. The Utama area on the western side of the site is where the Bale Timbang and pura are located, while the Nista area on the eastern side of the site holds the suites. Between the two areas is the Madya area, the centre for all activities, featuring the assembly room, restaurant, wellness facilities, and the meditation and yoga area. The distance between each function is quite close, with open green areas in between; this

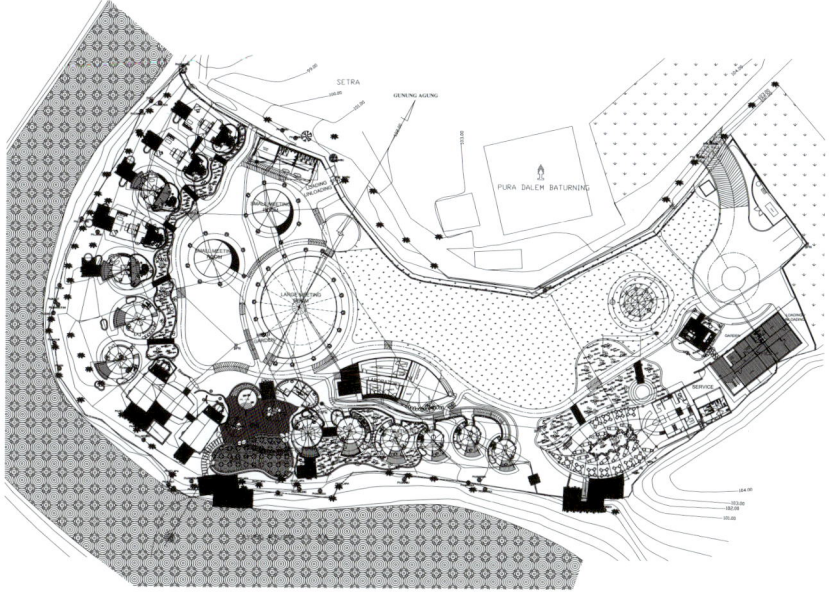

awakens in visitors the impression of traversing a traditional village of Bali. The most striking architectural element in the complex is the bamboo, which dominates each and every building. The most striking bamboo structure can be seen in the Mandala Agung building, situated in the area of Madya. This structure has a circular floor plan shaped like two fused shells. The architect applied 12-m-high bamboo arches with no columns in the middle of the structure. These bamboo arches are joined at the top and are supported by a bamboo cylinder that pierces the roof, creating a mountain-like construction. In addition to the Mandala Agung – the largest building in the area – similar structures are also found in several other buildings, albeit on a smaller scale.

Bamboe Koening Restaurant

112 C

Royal Casa Ganesha, Jalan Raya Lodtunduh, Ubud 80571
Effan Adhiwira
2013

Bamboe Koening Restaurant not only serves unique Indonesian dishes but also presents extraordinary bamboo architecture. An awareness of tropical architecture is illustrated by the construction of thousands of bamboo poles curved to shelter the wallless spaces underneath. To optimise natural air circulation and lighting, the whole construction is equipped with a layered roof that features gaps between the layers.

Gaya Fusion
Jalan Raya Sayan, Ubud, 80571
Arte Architect and Associates
1999

113 C

Stefano Grandi, an Italian businessman, and Nyoman Birit had the idea to create a representative space to contain the artistic talents of Bali and the world. This art space was then developed as a place for cultural exchange between many countries, complete with a resort facility. Both initiators appointed the Balinese architect Ketut Arthana of Arte Architect in collaboration with Filippo Sciascia. The initial idea dictated that an exhibition space should talk less than the works of art exhibited within. The most interesting feature of Gaya Fusion is that the architect designed two large stairways which are inspired by and adopted from Mayan temple architecture. These stairways are the main access leading to the building. On the exterior, palimanan sandstone is used as the finishing, projecting a sense of stability and solidity. The interior is a simple square-shaped area dominated by white and designed with a minimal number of columns and openings to achieve a high spatial flexibility.

Alila Ubud
Melinggih Kelod Village
Payangan, Gianyar 80572
Kerry Hill
1995

Poking out of the tropical forest of Bali, at first glance Alila Ubud resembles a tree house standing on the River Ayung. The accommodation that adopts the style of a resort consists of villas and rooms that are elevated, like houses on stilts perching on the edge of a cliff. Alila Ubud is equipped with an art gallery, gardens adorned with statues made by local artisans, and an infinity pool. Guests can enjoy the beautiful panorama of the forest and the sky from the pool. Kerry Hill, an Australian architect who established Kerry Hill Architects in Singapore, designed Alila Ubud by combining vernacular Balinese architecture into a modern geometric composition. The exploration of materials and the play on architectural styles are visible in the combination of smooth plaster walls and thatched roofs, the convergence of terrazzo floor and pebbles, and also the coupling of wood and glass.

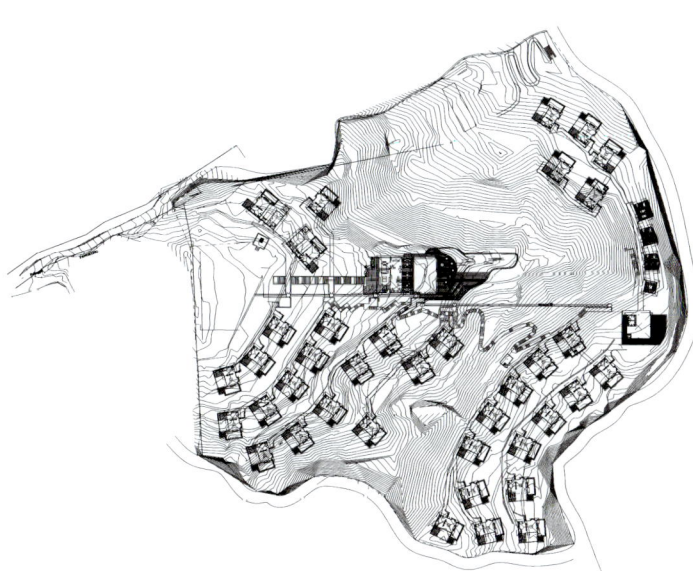

Ubud Hanging Gardens
Desa Buahan, Payangan
Gianyar 80571
Popo Danes Architect
2005

115 C

Ubud Hanging Gardens is a five-star boutique hotel located in the midst of paddy fields in Ubud, Bali. The hotel stands on a 3.2 ha contoured site. The architect Popo Danes divided the hotel into forty single-storey buildings, spread all over the site and following the contour of the land. The contour's steep landscape has the advantage of giving all buildings a stunning view, while also maintaining privacy.

An energy-saving building concept is the main idea behind Ubud Hanging Gardens. In each bedroom, the ceiling is tiered and the roof is thatched with cogon grass to lower the interior temperature. A verandah is also present as a buffer and open filter. Air conditioning is only used in 29 per cent of the hotel's total area, while artificial lighting is only used between 6–11 p.m and 5–6 a.m. These efforts are estimated to cut energy usage as much as 115.94 kWh per day. Popo Danes received the ASEAN Energy Awards 2008 for energy efficiency in the Tropical Building category for the design of Hanging Gardens Ubud.

In some areas in Bali, such as Ubud, stringent building regulations dictate that *alang-alang* (grass) must be used as a roofing material

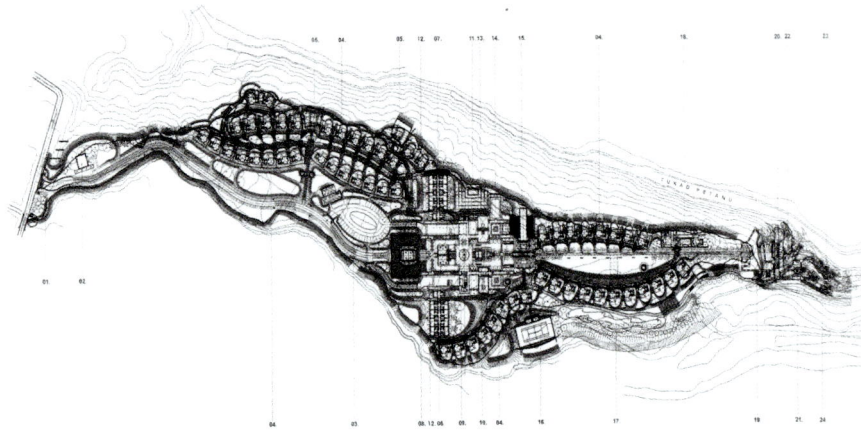

The Maya Ubud Resort and Spa

Jalan Gunung Sari Peliatan
Ubud 80571
Duta Cermat Mandiri
2001

116 C

The peninsula-shaped site – narrow at the front, wide in the middle, and tapering at the end – became the starting point of the design concept behind the Maya Ubud. This site is flanked by two rivers, the Pakerisan and the Petanu. The division into west-east wings is a unique design response to the condition of the site. These two wings protrude into the cottage area, given that the panoramas on these two sides are the most spectacular. The spa – which provides exceptional serenity and privacy – is located on the side of the site closest to the river. The design exploration, however, does not stop there. Distinctive touches of Balinese architecture are presented through thatched roofs, bamboo frames, and columns of coconut timber. An old wooden plow is reused as a part of the sofa and chaise longue, while old railway sleepers have been recycled into a table. The hotel, designed by DCM, was granted the main award in the Commercial Buildings category at the IAI Awards 2002.

Villa Bayad

Banjar Bayad, Payangan
Ubud 80572
Popo Danes Architect
2008

The strong point of Bayad Villa lies in the humbleness of its architectural design. Bayad Villa is situated at the top of a lush hill covered with terraced paddy fields in Payangan Village. The site is oriented to the east, towards the panorama of a pair of rice terraces flanking the river running below the villa. The villa complex consists of six buildings standing on a 7,500 m² area. The four bedroom units are clustered into two opposite groups. Additionally, the villa is also equipped with a common room, pendopo, and study – each located within a separate building, just like in traditional Balinese houses. Most of the buildings in the Villa Bayad complex are designed as open buildings supported by wooden or concrete columns. These buildings are interconnected through gazebos and corridors. The open building design is synergised with the outdoor landscape which the site owes its lushness to, resulting in a dynamic dialogue between the indoor and outdoor areas. Even though the design of the buildings is very open, Popo Danes successfully made the most of the site's contour and arranged the orientation of the buildings so as to maintain the privacy of Villa Bayad's guests.

Puri Wulandari
Jalan Raya Kedewatan
Ubud 80571
Arte Architect and Associates
1999

Puri Wulandari is a boutique hotel that was designed to maximise the serene environment of Ubud. Puri Wulandari is located 650 m from the nearest main thoroughfare, with an access road flanked by paddy fields. On the contoured site, Ketut Arthana of Arte Architect arranged the functions based on the height of the contour. The lobby, located on the highest contour, was designed as a building surrounded by water, akin to the Kerta Gosa at Klungkung. The open lobby also provides a breathtaking view of the Ayung River to the greenery beyond. For the villa area, the architect planned the area as a layered cluster that resembles a bow adapted to the contour of the site. The cluster, consisting of single units of villas, is oriented to the east with its back to the Tukad Ayung River on the lower west side. As with Balinese traditional villages, between the villa units there are courtyards with interconnecting footpaths so that the spatial continuity is easily discernible.

Valley scenery from Puri Wulandari

Other Islands

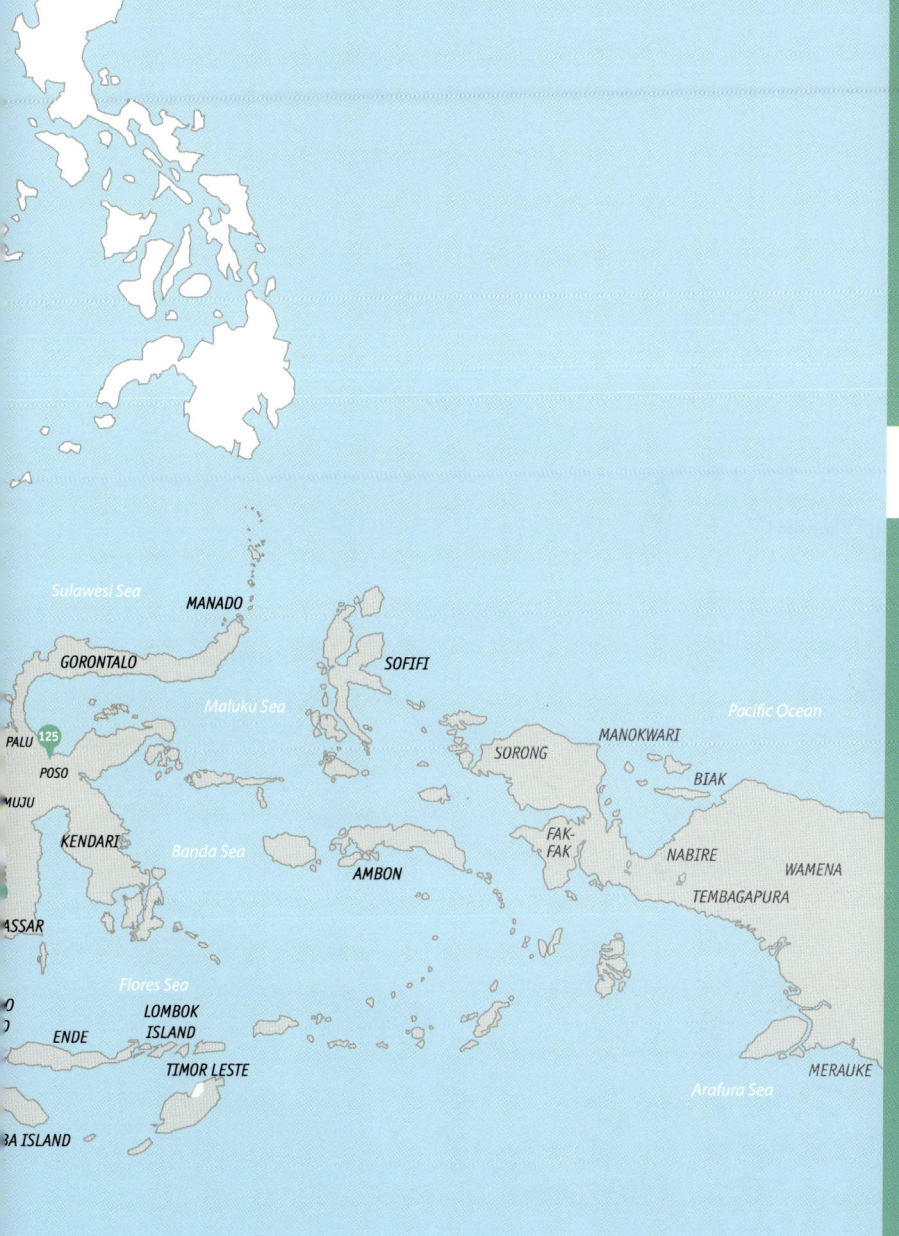

The landscape of Aceh

Post-tsunami Architecture in Sumatra

Dita Kusumawardhani

Sumatra is one of the islands located on the western part of Indonesia. It is a 473,481 km² island, hailed as the sixth largest island in the world. From its northern tip to its southern end, the island is adorned with lakes of unparalleled beauty. Lakes Ancuelot and Laut Tawar in Nanggroe Aceh Darussalam, Lake Toba in North Sumatra, Lake Singkarak and Lake Maninjau in West Sumatra, Lake Matana in South Sumatra, Lake Emas (gold) in Bengkulu, and Lake Jepara in Lampung are only a few examples of the lakes spread all over Sumatra.

Its size and natural beauty are not the only factors that make Sumatra famous. The island is also well known for its abundant natural resources, such as oil palms, tobacco, petroleum, tin, bauxite, coal, and natural gas. According to the data obtained from the official website of the Republic of Indonesia, the mining area covers no less than 1,030,128.75 ha. Besides mining, agriculture is also one of the economic pillars that are burgeoning in this island. In the South Sumatra province, for instance, the area reserved for agriculture reaches 5,524.725 ha, equal to 70 per cent of the total area of South Sumatra. This projection confirms that the majority of Sumatra is used for mining or agriculture.

Despite having fertile land and abundant minerals, as well as other mining products, Sumatra is not without its shortcomings. The island is one of those in Indonesia most vulnerable to natural disasters. Geographically, three main tectonic plates in the world converge in Indonesia, namely in Sumatra, Java, Bali, Nusa Tenggara, Maluku, Sulawesi, and Papua. The continental crust in the western parts of Indonesia, the Eurasian Plate, moves in an east-southeast direction at a speed of 1 cm per year. In the southern part of Indonesia, the continental and oceanic crust of the Australian-Indian Plate moves to the north at a speed of 7 cm per year. Meanwhile, in the eastern part of Indonesia, the oceanic crust of the Pacific Plate moves in a west-northwest direction at a speed of 9 cm per year.

In December 2004, for instance, the continental crust located 30 km under the Sumatran seas shifted, resulting in a 9.2 Mw earthquake. The shift triggered tsunami waves of up to 30 m high that reached a speed of 500 km per hour. This force is equal to 23,000 Hiroshima bombs. The tsunami supposedly swept 800 km of coastline and hit the western and southern parts of Aceh – Banda Aceh, Aceh Besar, Aceh Jaya, and Aceh Barat – and Simeulue Island. According to the *BRR* book series, in Banda Aceh, capital of the Nanggroe Aceh Darussalam province, around 800,000 ha of land was swept clean by the tsunami. In the town of Lhoknga, Aceh Besar, the disaster left only seven hundred out of the six thousand people living there. In total, the tsunami caused 167,799 deaths and destroyed around 500,000 homes. Five years later, another earthquake – with a magnitude of 7.6 on the Richter scale – occurred off the coast of West Sumatra. This earthquake also claimed many victims and a number of buildings collapsed as a result of it, although it was not as severe as the one that hit Aceh previously.

The fatal tsunami disaster brought a number of impacts towards the construction sector of Sumatra. In Aceh, post-disaster buildings built by various parties from both inside and outside of Indonesia were erected. This post-disaster architecture brought new nuances to Aceh. In 2009 the Tsunami Commemoration Museum was constructed. The museum's design was the result of a nation-wide design competition won by Urbane, an architectural firm based in Bandung, West Java. The museum was built to commemorate the tsunami disaster that hit Aceh in 2004.

Other contemporary architecture also emerged, such as the Novotel Palembang designed by Duta Cermat Mandiri. This was followed by Timmy Setiawan's design for Surau Baitul Djalil in Bukittinggi, West Sumatra. In 2011, foreign architects began to take part; TYIN Tegnestue Architects from Norway designed the Cassia Co-op Training Centre in Jambi. In 2014, RAW and Urbane increasingly intensified the architectural field in Sumatra by designing Arumdalu Resort in Belitung and the Grand Mosque of West Sumatra in Padang.

The government's plan regarding the construction of the Trans-Sumatra highway stretching from Lampung to Aceh would no doubt lead to a lot of conveniences

An electricity generator barge was swept away by the tsunami into a village 10 km away and destroyed many buildings: now the barge informally acts as a *museum*

in the various sectors that require land transportation. The high increase in the infrastructure networks would not only increase the numbers in the tourism sector, but also become a generator for the development of the construction sector. Given that the island already possesses copious amounts of natural resources, the increase in the quality of the infrastructure of Sumatra would only make the island a fertile ground for the growth of contemporary architecture. And it would mean that architecture in Indonesia would progress much more evenly in every region.

In contrast to Java, half of Sumatra's mountains are still covered with thick tropical rainforest due to unequal economic development

D

Most cities in Sumatra have expanded without proper city planning

For the last five years, Bukittinggi – a mountainous resort in West Sumatra – has experienced an abrupt rise in population: the population of the nearby waterfront city Padang has increasingly moved there to avoid earthquakes

The Growth of Architecture on the Other Islands of Indonesia

Dita Kusumawardhani

Indonesia, also known as Nusantara, comprises about seventeen thousand islands. Besides Java, Bali, and Sumatra, thousands of other islands have also been bestowed with unparalleled natural beauty. The Derawan Islands in Kalimantan, Labuan Bajo and Komodo Island in East Nusa Tenggara, and the Raja Ampat Islands in West Papua, famous for their underwater charm, are but a few examples of these islands' – henceforth referred to as the Other Islands – beauty. Moreover, these Other Islands also hold significant natural resources. Kalimantan, the third largest island in the world, is famous for its sizable rainforest areas. According to the South Kalimantan Province website, in 2013 the size of the rainforest in South Kalimantan alone covered an area of 8,562,287 ha, or equal to 69.8 times the total land area of Bali. Kalimantan, the *Island of A Thousand Rivers*, is also well known for its riverside civilization. No less than sixty-seven rivers on this island have attracted people to live and obtain their livelihood along their watersheds. Unlike any other cultures found throughout Indonesia's numerous islands, in Kalimantan the activities of trading and transporting are mostly conducted on the river, since the natives of Kalimantan believe that rivers are the water of life. Even today we can see these floating houses and markets on the rivers of Kalimantan.

East of Kalimantan is Sulawesi Island, whose shape roughly resembles the letter *K*. On this island, a variety of mining produce – iron, copper, gold, silver, nickel, titanium, manganese, iron sand, sulfur, and many others – is available in abundance. Further east, the islands of Maluku, West Papua and Nusa Tenggara boast a unique and rich biodiversity. The splendour of the undersea ecosystem, exotic beaches, diverse flora and fauna, and the panoramic beauty of the mountain ranges found on the Other Islands should be reason enough for these islands to become a potential for tourism to be developed and maintained. But alas, behind the beautiful appearance of the Other Islands is an age-old problem which began under the regime of Suharto,

Riverside houses like these can be found on many rivers in Kalimantan

the New Order Regime (1966–1998). Under this regime, the economy of Indonesia was focused not far from the administrative centres of each region. The top-down system which was applied to every aspect of Indonesia's development only served to emphasise economic stability around the centres of the regional government. These centres were almost entirely controlled by the central government residing in Jakarta. Ironically, this centralisation system was not only applied to governmental and economic policies, but also to the national development agendas.

This inequality also affected the construction sector. The development of infrastructure outside of Java was severely delayed compared to the much more developed Java. Electricity, clean water, sanitation, and adequate road networks are some of the problems that persist on the Other Islands even now. It is no surprise that these islands have very little to offer in terms of architectural achievements.

Laying the basis of development that is equitable on every aspect in every region is not an easy feat, especially for a country with a geographic, demographic, and geopolitical diversity like Indonesia. The passing of the Regional Autonomy Law in 1999 gradually brought a bright spot that may solve the problem in the construction sector on Indonesia's Other Islands. The strong support from the current government is another plus point. For instance, the Manado-Bitung highway was inaugurated in October 2014 in Sulawesi. The 39-km-long toll road connects Manado with the development centre of the Bitung Special Economic Zone. Even so, these shortcomings and hindrances do not necessarily mean that these islands are untouched by the creative hands of architects. The works of young architects such as Yu Sing from Bandung and Effan Adhiwira, the bamboo specialist architect from Yogyakarta, not only prove that contemporary architects have stepped out farther than the capital city, but have also successfully inspired many others to do so. Observe the Phinisi Tower of UNM in Makassar, South Sulawesi, designed by Yu Sing. The tower soon became one of the icons of Makassar. In the meantime, Effan Adhiwira, whose mission it is to raise the value of bamboo in the eyes of the world, inspired many architects through his exploration of bamboo material in the Almarik Hotel Restaurant in Lombok, West Nusa Tenggara, and his exploration of indigenous materials in the Dodoha Mosintuwu building in Poso, Central Sulawesi. If the plan to develop the infrastructure on these Other Islands runs smoothly, the development of architecture on these islands is expected to grow rapidly. However, let us hope that the development will not be as sporadic as in Java.

Floating market in Kalimantan

The scenery of the Komodo Islands will change dramatically within five years as they become a favourite tourist destination and grow rapidly: for instance, these two fishing boats will be converted into tourist boats to keep up with the tourism demand

Komodo National Park has become a popular destination in the last two years after UNESCO declared the island a World Heritage Site

Novotel Palembang

Jalan Sukamto No. 8A Palembang
South Sumatera 30127
Duta Cermat Mandiri
2003

119 D

Celebrating the greatness of the Sriwijaya Empire is the concept behind the design for Novotel Palembang. The Sriwijaya Empire, which began its existence in Palembang in the seventh century, constructed magnificent architecture. The historical records stored in Palembang became the great idea behind the hotel's design, an idea developed by the DCM architectural firm into a monumental garden that would remind guests of the magnificent architecture of Sriwijaya Empire. The garden was realised in the shape of a circular mandala whose diameter measures 100 m and was designed as the central axis of the hotel. Constructed around it are ninety-eight gigantic pillars measuring 4.8 m x 4.8 m with a height of 12 m. The garden mandala is equipped with a circular corridor that is connected to the room area. A quick glance at the interior reveals the presence of Arabic and Chinese cultures which are very influential in Palembang. The resort-style business hotel consists of 138 rooms, forty-four apartment units, and two penthouses.

Arumdalu Eco Resort
Jalan Batu Lubang, Membalong
Belitung 33452
RAW
2014

Arumdalu Eco Resort is a private deluxe resort located on the southwest area of Belitung. The resort offers cosy accommodation with a serene panorama of the surrounding beaches and forest. It consists of ten villas with luxurious facilities, such as a private pool, gazebo, and outdoor shower for each villa. The resort is also equipped with a café called the Sahang Beachfront Café and Resto, as well as a spa. Rumah Pintar Arumdalu (Arumdalu Smart Home), which is located within the premises of the resort, empowers local communities surrounding Arumdalu to create local artwork such as batiks. Visitors are encouraged to meet and greet local batik artists and learn to create their own versions. Designed to be an eco-friendly and self-sustaining property, the resort utilises local materials for its buildings and furniture, transforms seaweed into fertiliser, treats wastewater for reuse, and also uses the heat from air-conditioning units to heat water.

Cassia Co-op Training Centre

Desa Koto Dumo, Tanah Kampung
Jambi 37100
TYIN Tegnestue Architects
2003

121 D

The idea behind this training centre began when Patrick Barthelemy, a French cinnamon businessman who believes that 85 per cent of the cinnamon consumed in the world originates from Sumatra, visited the office of TYIN Tegnestue Architects in Trondheim, Norway. The need to change the overall disregard for the rights of the workers, to improve minimum safety and health precautions, and to address inadequate pay was the drive behind the establishment of the Cassia Co-op Training Centre. The owner challenged the architect to create natural air circulation, reduce sunlight, and make the eaves function optimally. The architect then began with the classic concept of combining brick, wood, and concrete. TYIN Architects used the bricks to form the walls, and the Y-shaped wooden structure was set on a concrete foundation to support the roof and wide eaves. Cassia Co-op Training Centre, which is situated in Desa Koto Dumo in Jambi, is now a school and training centre for local cinnamon farmers and workers.

Surau Baitul Djalil
Jalan Janjang 40, Bukittinggi
West Sumatera 26113
Timmy Setiawan
2005

A house of worship, capable of holding 250 worshippers, built in the midst of a crowded market has become an oasis at the centre of Bukittinggi, West Sumatra. The all-white Surau Baitul Djalil (*surau* or *musholla* is a house of worship generally smaller than a mosque) was designed by the architect Timmy Setiawan chock full of cultural references. However, unlike traditional Minang houses which are resplendent with their bagonjong roofs, on Surau Baitul Djalil the bagonjong roof comes in silhouettes. Four bagonjong roofs meet at the centre of the main space, the prayer area measuring 11 m x 11 m, creating an image of a blooming flower. A glass-covered slit was created at each corner of the roof to allow natural light to penetrate the interior. Surau Baitul Djalil was recognised at the 2011 IAI Awards in the Public Building category.

Mahligai Minang Mosque
Jalan Khatib Sulaiman
Padang, West Sumatera 25137
Urbane Indonesia
2015

Mahligai Minang is the grand mosque of West Sumatera representing a total floor area of 18,000 m². The largest mosque in Indonesia was the result of a design competition held in 2007. Rizal Muslimin, an architect from PT Urbane Indonesia and the principal designer of Mahligai Minang, proposed a design which was to be a metaphor for a desert tent whose four corners are supported by tent poles, so that the points are tapered upwards. Because of these pointed corners, the mosque is often thought to be inspired by the traditional homes of the Minangkabau, whose shape is similar. The main function of the mosque is elevated one level above ground, while the area below is used as public area filled with thematic gardens. Besides the mosque, there are other supporting masses accommodating a community centre, commercial area and an Islamic school.

Mahligai Minang Mosque's form is derived from a fusion between vernacular and modern architecture in a single building

Tsunami Commemoration Museum

Jalan Sultan Iskandar Muda
Banda Aceh, Aceh 23125
Urbane Indonesia
2009

Tsunami Commemoration Museum is a museum built to memorialise the tsunami disaster that hit Aceh in 2004. The building adopts the traditional Aceh structure of a house on stilts and consists of four storeys. Inspired by the shape of a whirlpool, the building is shaped in a curve, while its skin is inspired by the traditional dance of Aceh, the Saman dance. The floor plan of the ground and first floors of the museum is elliptical, while the second and third floors' floor plan consists of two connecting curves that form a void at the centre. On the roof of the building is a garden that functions as an evacuation area, should a flood or another tsunami hit the area in the future. The movement sequence inside the museum is designed to arouse the visitor's psychological sensitivity and recollect the tsunami disaster of 2004, beginning from the Spaces of Memory area, then leading through the Tsunami Passage, the Memorial Hall, the Blessing Chamber, the Light of Hope, the Atrium of Hope, before ending on the roof of the building.

Dodoha Mosintuwu

Jalan Raya Yosi, Pamona
Poso 94663
Effan Adhiwira
2009

Dodoha Mosintuwu is the headquarters of Mosintuwu Insitute, an NGO fighting to secure peace and sovereignty for people living in the post-conflict area of Poso, Central Sulawesi. Located in Pamona, Central Sulawesi, the building consists of a multipurpose hall, library, pantry, and bedrooms for volunteers, as well as an office. The hall, located on the front side of the building, is frequently used for meetings and NGO events, and also functions as a restaurant serving local Pamona dishes. The headquarters also accommodates inspirational facilities such as a school for women, children's library, and community space. The dominant bamboo structure is combined with brick walls to create a large library with a diameter of 8 m. Bamboo, bricks, and thatch – which is used for the roof – are materials easily found around the site, therefore reducing the carbon footprint of the building.

Almarik Hotel Restaurant
Gili Trawangan, Pemenang
Lombok 83352
Effan Adhiwira
2013

Almarik Hotel Restaurant is designed as an eco-conscious building. The iconic and spacious seaside restaurant with an optimised capacity is sheltered from glaring sunlight and torrential rain. The result is curved bamboo structures which are floored with beach sand and covered with a lightweight roofing material. Situated on the coastline of Gili Trawangan, Lombok, the building was designed by following local rules in terms of its development, including the prohibiting of engined vehicles and large machinery. The rules also dictated that the building on the coastline was to be be semi-permanent and use lightweight roofing materials. The dining room is designed with no columns, thus maximising the view towards Gili Trawangan Beach. To reach the column-free dining room, an 18-m-long bamboo structure was built to mimic the shape of flip-flops. While the dining room is floored with natural beach sand, a wooden deck has been constructed in the lounge. The terraced roof is festooned with gaps to anticipate the wind load from the sea. Architect Effan Adhiwira demonstrates here that the combination of bamboo structures and fabric represents his materials of choice for the roof.

Pinisi Tower UNM
Jalan Andi Pangerang Pettarani
Makassar
Sulawesi Selatan
akanoma
2014

127 D

The design for this seventeen-storey building was chosen as the winner of a design competition for the Academic Service Centre of Universitas Negeri Makassar (UNM). Blending philosophy, culture, and traditional architecture with a modern context is the fundamental concept behind this building. Pinisi Tower is divided into three areas: *rakkaena* (head), *lotang* (body) and *awa bola* (pit). Today, the building is widely recognised as being the new icon of UNM.

Vernacular Architecture in Indonesia

Traditional houses of Ratenggaro Village being rebuilt

The Future of Vernacular Architecture in Indonesia

Alicchys Siregar

Indonesia consists of more than 560 ethnic groups and seventeen thousand islands. Even today, some of these ethnic groups still live in traditional houses in traditional villages located in remote areas, adhering to the customs inherited by their ancestors since time immemorial. A lot of these vernacular villages have been eroded by – or altogether disappeared with – the passage of time, or have been assimilated by modernity. However, there are still some among them which have chosen to preserve their traditions.

Of those which preserve their traditions, most are on the verge of extinction due to several causes. First, almost all cases relating to the disappearance of indigenous villages are triggered by one thing: fire. The main materials used for building houses in any of these villages are predominantly the same: wood, bamboo, reeds and *ijuk* (palm tree fibres) – all of which are very vulnerable to fire. Second, the severely limited economic conditions of these villages mercilessly hamper the villagers' ability to preserve their traditions – and sometimes political and social conditions also threaten their existence. Third, the lack of public – and government – awareness and effort in preserving Indonesian cultures, especially the traditional houses. And finally, almost nonexistent documentation due to the fact that most traditional cultures of Indonesia are cultures of oral tradition. Any documentation of these cultures therefore vanished since they were not inherited in written texts.

Luckily, in the past few years several architects who are greatly agitated with this condition have begun to preserve these traditional villages. The Rumah Asuh Foundation, founded in 2008 by the architect Yori Antar, seeks to assist people to rebuild traditional houses. This movement is largely supported by the philanthropist Lisa Tirto Utomo, together with her Tirto Utomo Foundation that focuses on helping traditional communities in Indonesia. To obtain assistance from the Runah Asuh Foundation, three requirements must be met: first, that the locals are actually living in accordance with long-standing local traditions; second, the traditional houses or buildings to be preserved or restored are needed for the continuation of the tradition; and third, the construction of such buildings must be conducted traditionally and hand in hand with the local people. Yori Antar thus describes this activity as building a living culture. Several young architects and students of architecture were assigned to record and document each step of the construction process in the hope that traditional architecture could be studied and scrutinised by a larger number of people through photography, essays, articles, and films. The reconstruction of five traditional houses in Wae Rebo, Flores, won the 2012 UNESCO Asia-Pacific Award for Cultural Heritage Conservation. The movement attracted more parties, and now several young architects, such as Mukhlis Mohtar from Flores, Mohammad Cahyo from Surabaya, Eko Alvarez from Padang, and other donors have followed suit.

The effort to rebuild traditional houses is not just owing to reasons related to nostalgia or a recollection of the past, but is an effort to respond to the needs of local communities. This movement eventually contributed to the empowerment of local communities and the revival of traditional culture. Moreover, the architects also help the locals to make their indigenous villages accessible to tourists through eco-tourism approaches.

The record of the process of rebuilding the traditional houses has become the most comprehensive documentation on vernacular architecture of Indonesia. This knowledge is a most precious treasure for future generations, both in local communities and the academic world. The availability of this comprehensive documentation is what allows us to present traditional houses in Wae Rebo, Sumba, Nias, and Nagari Sumpu as a special section within this architectural guide.

Traditional houses of Wae Rebo rebuilt

Reconstruction of Uma Pangembe of Wainyapu
Wainyapu, Southwest Sumba, East Nusa Tenggara
Society of Wainyapu (supervised by Yori Antar/Rumah Asuh Foundation)
2012

For the people of Wainyapu, the reconstruction of their traditional houses was tantamount to the reconstruction of their lost identity. Around thirty traditional houses in Wainyapu had been destroyed by natural disasters, and these houses were where the people of Wainyapu performed their religious rituals. Without these traditional houses, this was impossible. However, since 2012 dozens of traditional houses have been reconstructed and Wainyapu is once again filled with its own version of skyscrapers, such as the Uma Pangembe (literally Tower House), which is entirely built of wood and covered with a thatched roof. In common with construction processes in other traditional villages, the reconstruction of Uma Pangembe also overflowed with communal activities and mutual help. According to the people of Wainyapu, mutual help is a tremendous strength that must be preserved.[1]

[1] Robin Hartanto, Kilas Karya Budaya, Jejak Sewindu Yayasan Tirto Utomo (Jakarta: Yayasan Tirto Utomo, 2013) 39.

Reconstruction of Uma Pangembe of Ratenggaro
Ratenggaro, Southwest Sumba, East Nusa Tenggara
Society of Ratenggaro (supervised by Yori Antar/Rumah Asuh Foundation)
2011

The traditional village of Ratenggaro is located right across from the Wainyapu traditional village, separated by the estuary of the River Waiha. The traditional houses in Ratenggaro are also towering constructions, whose rooftops are almost as high as a five-storey building (taller than the traditional houses in Wainyapu). The height of the roof signifies wealth and closeness to the divine. In 2011, some of these traditional houses were reconstructed in order to replace the thirteen houses destroyed by fire in June 2004. During reconstruction, the workers created a magnificent spectacle as they attached the reeds that cover the roof of the house. The reeds were tied in bundles and thrown to workers clinging on to the frame of the roof who then attached the bundle of reeds to the frame. With every throw, exuberant cries resounded from the mouth of each villager involved in the reconstruction process.

Reconstruction of a North Nias House

North Nias, North Sumatra
Society of North Nias (supervised by Yori Antar/ Rumah Asuh Foundation)
2010

In North Nias a traditional house, or Omo Hada, is normally classified as a *laraga*: an oval-shaped stilt house. Similar to other traditional housing types found in Nias (the *gomo* and *lasara* types), laraga-type houses are also supported by a log structure in diagonal and vertical arrangement. The structure helps these houses to avoid massive damage caused by earthquakes, especially since the wooden structure stands on a stone foundation (the structure is not embedded into the ground). Its resistance to earthquake forces was evident when a massive earthquake hit Nias on 28 March 2005. Even though some traditional houses were damaged, it was more likely caused by their age. However, according to records, no inhabitants of these traditional houses became victims to the earthquake. The reconstruction of these traditional North Nias houses was conducted as a response to the fact that these houses are now a rarity.

Reconstruction of a South Nias House

South Nias, North Sumatra
*Society of South Nias
(supervised by Yori Antar/
Rumah Asuh Foundation)*
2010

The traditional houses of South Nias belong to the lasara type. Unlike the oval laraga-type houses, a lasara is a rectangular house extended to the rear. In the traditional village of Bawömataluo (the name means the *Land of the Sun*) in South Nias, these traditional houses stand side by side in two rows which flank the main road for hundreds of metres. It is in this village that the unique feature of this traditional house, the skylight (which is noticeably absent in any other type of traditional house in Indonesia), can be seen neatly lined up. One example of a lasara-type traditional house to have been reconstructed is the Omo Sebua, or the grand traditional house of Hilimondregeraya Village. In addition to its function as a home, the 8.5 m x 12 m house is also the venue for important village events, such as village gatherings and traditional ceremonies.

Reconstruction of Rumah Gadang of Nagari Sumpu

Sumpur, West Sumatra
Society of Sumpur (supervised by Yori Antar and Eko Alvarez Z.)
2014

132 E

Rumah Gadang (literally, grand house) is the traditional house of Minangkabau, an ethnic group originating from West Sumatra. The house functions as a venue for traditional ceremonies and forum sessions, and also as a home. The unique features of Rumah Gadang are the sharp gables at each end of the house that resemble the horns of a water buffalo (*atap bagonjong*) and the curved walls that make the house resemble a boat. Rumah Gadang are owned by several families, and the right to a Rumah Gadang, as well as the basic concept behind its rooms, is matrilineal. The reconstruction of the Rumah Gadang in Nagari Sumpu began after the houses were severely damaged by a fire on 26 May 2013. The disaster destroyed five Rumah Gadang, each one more than a hundred years old. Eko Alvarez and Yori Antar initiated the effort in an attempt to turn Nagari Sumpu into a heritage site.

Wae Rebo Reconstruction

Wae Rebo Village, Manggarai
East Nusa Tenggara
Society of Wae Rebo
*(supervised by Rumah Asuh Foundation /
Han Awal & Partners)*
2010

Wae Rebo is a traditional village located on top of a hill surrounded by mountainous areas 1,100–1,200 m above sea level. Its remote location is the reason why a trip to Wae Rebo is very complex: the visitor must first fly by plane to Denpasar, Bali, then to Labuan Bajo, Flores, before continuing the journey by ferry to Aimere, then by car to Dengedan village in Ruteng, before finally trekking to Wae Rebo. The director of Han Awal & Partners, Yori Antar, and his colleagues accidentally *discovered* this village in 2008. At that time only four of the seven traditional houses – *mbaru niang* – were standing, while three of the seven houses were heavily damaged. Knowing this, the Rumah Asuh Foundation – which was founded by Yori Antar – was motivated to encourage Wae Rebo villagers to rebuild their damaged mbaru niang, funded by the Tirto Utomo Foundation. The mbaru niang is a cone-shaped house consisting of five floors with different functions. It is supported by a main column (*saka*) of worok wood taken from the surrounding forest. The roof of a mbaru niang is made of palm fibre and reeds. The first reconstructed house was completed in 2009 within the space of four months. The second house was completed in 2010, involving several architectural students and young architects who had studied the process of building a traditional house. More than just rebuilding, the reconstruction of mbaru niang is a process of knowledge transfer handed down from generation to generation so that villagers can rebuild their own house if it is damaged at a later date. To make the whole process accessible to the public, the reconstruction was documented in books and videos. Before reaching Wae Rebo, tourists can visit the Information Centre and Library of Wae Rebo in Denge. Since information on Wae Rebo reaches a wider audience, villagers can now earn additional income from ecotourism, besides farming.

Wae Rebo Village, situated amidst pleasant and isolated mountain scenery

Appendix

Index of Buildings

#
088	1903 Restaurant	227

A
049	Administration Centre of University of Indonesia	133
065	Al Irsyad Mosque	184
114	Alila Ubud	311
108	Alila Villas Soori	297
099	Alila Villas Uluwatu	279
126	Almarik Hotel Restaurant	358
067	Amanjiwo Hotel	188
096	Amarterra Villas	270
020	Anjung Salihara	86
120	Arumdalu Eco Resort	346
009	ASEAN Secretariat	68

B
006	Bakoel Koffie	62
014	Bakrie Tower	76
097	The Bale	275
112	Bamboe Koening Restaurant	307
079	Bank Indonesia Solo	210
080	Bank Indonesia Solo (Extension)	213
033	Bank Indonesia Thamrin	112
005	Bina Nusantara International School	61
002	Bina Nusantara University	54
092	Blimbingsari Airport Banyuwangi	236
052	Bogor Raya School	139
054	Breeze Art and Boutique Hotel	163
074	Bumi Pemuda Rahayu	197

C
025	Café Batavia	97
121	Cassia Coop Training Centre	348
070	Cemeti Art House	191
050	Central Library of University of Indonesia	134
053	Cikampek Rest Area	141
057	Concordia	169
095	Conrad Wedding Chapel	269

D
087	De Soematra	224
015	Dia.Lo.Gue Artspace	79
125	Dodoha Mosintuwu	357
031	DPR/MPR Parliament Building	108
064	Dusun Bambu	183

F
111	Fivelements Puri Ahimsa Healing Centre	303

G
021	Galeri Salihara	89
113	Gaya Fusion	398
029	Gedung Arsip Nasional	103
008	Gedung Yohanes, Church of St. John the Evangelist	66
012	Gelora Bung Karno Main Stadium	74
010	Graha Niaga	71
110	Green School	300
071	Greenhost Boutique Hotel	192
094	Guest House Banyuwangi	239
063	Gupondoro	181

H
048	Hall of University of Indonesia	132
045	The Hermitage	126
089	Historica Coffee and Pastry	229
026	Historical Museum of Jakarta	97
037	Hotel Indonesia	118
090	Hotel Majapahit	231

I
086	Intiland Tower Surabaya	222
032	Istiqlal Mostique	109
101	Ize Hotel	282

J
081	Javaplant	215

K
042	Kampus Semanggi Universitas Atma Jaya Jakarta	124
017	Kemang 89	83
047	Kementrian Perdagangan Republik Indonesia	130
018	Komunitas Salihara	84
035	Kosenda Hotel	114

M
123	Mahligai Minang Mosque	351
013	Manhattan Hotel	76

076	Maria Regina School	203	**S**	
038	Masjid Said Naum	118	019	Salihara Office	84
105	Maya Sanur	292	059	Salman Mosque, ITB	172
116	The Maya Ubud Resort and Spa	317	082	Santa Maria Assumpta Church	216
043	Metropole Cinema	124	003	Sekolah Terpadu Pa Hoa	55
109	Millenium Bridge	298	062	Selasar Sunaryo Art Space	176
034	Monumen Nasional	112	075	Sendangsono Pilgrimage Complex	200
046	Morissey Hotel	129	055	Sensa Hotel	164
004	Multimedia Nusantara University	56	011	Sequis Centre	73
027	Museum of Bank Indonesia	98	001	Soekarno Hatta Airport	52
028	Museum of Bank Mandiri	100	084	Soekarno Memorial Park	220
091	Musholla Kompleks Banyuwangi	232	131	South Nias House (Reconstruction)	273
	N		030	Stella Maris Catholic Church	105
072	Nasirun Gallery	194	104	Sudamala Suites	290
073	Ngibikan Village Reconstruction	196	122	Surau Baitul Djalil	350
130	North Nias House (Reconstruction)	371		**T**	
119	Novotel Palembang	345	007	Talavera Office Park	65
056	Nu Ciwalk	166	106	Tandjung Sari Hotel	293
098	Nusa Dua Tourism Project	276	022	Teater Salihara	90
			124	Tsunami Commemoration Museum	354
	O		085	Hotel Tugu	221
103	Oasis Lagoon Sanur	288	044	Tugu Kunstkring Paleis	125
068	Oei Hong Djien Museum	189			
024	Omah Architecture Library	96		**U**	
083	Open Museum of Trowulan Archaeological Site	218	115	Ubud Hanging Gardens	313
066	Outward Bound Indonesia	186	129	Uma Pangembe of Ratenggaro (Reconstruction)	368
	P		128	Uma Pangembe of Wainyapu (Reconstruction)	366
058	Padma Hotel	170	040	UOB Plaza	121
016	The Papilion	81			
093	Pendopo Bupati Banyuwangi	236		**V**	
127	Pinisi Tower UNM	359	069	Via Via Café Yogyakarta	190
051	Plaza Quantum Elektro FTUI	138	102	Villa Alopa	286
107	Popo Danes Studio	294	117	Villa Bayad	318
100	Potato Head Beach Club Restaurant	280			
118	Puri Wulandari	321		**W**	
			133	Wae Rebo (Reconstruction)	377
	R		060	West and East Halls of ITB	173
132	Rumah Gadang of Nagari Sumpu (Reconstruction)	375	023	West One Marketing Office	92
077	Rumah Rempah Karya	207	039	Wisma BNI	120
078	Rumah Turi	209	041	Wisma Dharmala	123
061	Rumah#1	175	036	Wisma Nusantara	116

Index of Architects

A
Abel Sorensen
037 Hotel Indonesia 118
Aboday
046 Morissey Hotel 129
Achmad Noe'man
060 West and East Halls of ITB 173
Adhi Moersid
038 Masjid Said Naum 118
Adi Purnomo
094 Guest House Banyuwangi 239
076 Maria Regina School 203
093 Pendopo Bupati Banyuwangi 236
003 Sekolah Terpadu Pa Hoa 55
022 Teater Salihara 90
Airmas Asri
007 Talavera Office Park 65
akanoma
127 Pinisi Tower UNM 359
andramatin
006 Bakoel Koffie 62
092 Blimbingsari Airport Banyuwangi 236
095 Conrad Wedding Chapel 269
015 Dia.Lo.Gue Artspace 79
081 Javaplant 215
091 Musholla Kompleks Banyuwangi 232
100 Potato Head Beach Club Restaurant 280
019 Salihara Office 84
Andry Widyowijatnoko
066 Outward Bound Indonesia 186
APTA
064 Dusun Bambu 183
Arte Architect and Associates
111 Fivelements Puri Ahimsa Healing Centre 303
113 Gaya Fusion 398
118 Puri Wulandari 321

B
Bali Tourism Development Corporation (BTDC)
098 Nusa Dua Tourism Project 276
Bambang Setia Budi and Team
059 Salman Mosque, ITB 172
PT Bamboo Pure
110 Green School 300
109 Millenium Bridge 298

Baskoro Tedjo
062 Selasar Sunaryo Art Space 176
084 Soekarno Memorial Park 220
Boy Bhirawa
026 Historical Museum of Jakarta (Restoration) 97
Budi A. Sukada
048 Hall of University of Indonesia 132
Budi Lim
048 Gedung Arsip Nasional (Restoration) 103

D
d-associates
053 Cikampek Rest Area 141
068 Oei Hong Djien Museum 189
016 The Papilion 81
Djoko Kusumowidagdo
066 Outward Bound Indonesia 186
Duta Cermat Mandiri
005 Bina Nusantara International School 61
002 Bina Nusantara University 54
050 Central Library of University of Indonesia 134
047 Kementrian Perdagangan Republik Indonesia 130
013 Manhattan Hotel 76
105 Maya Sanur 292
116 The Maya Ubud Resort and Spa 317
004 Multimedia Nusantara University 56
119 Novotel Palembang 345
056 Nu Ciwalk 166
055 Sensa Hotel 164
030 Stella Maris Catholic Church 105
085 Hotel Tugu 221
040 UOB Plaza 121

E
E. S. A. International
104 Sudamala Suites 290
Ed Tuttle
067 Amanjiwo Hotel 188
Eduard Cuypers
079 Bank Indonesia Solo 210
Effan Adhiwira
126 Almarik Hotel Restaurant 358
112 Bamboe Koening Restaurant 307

074	Bumi Pemuda Rahayu	197	058	Padma Hotel	170
125	Dodoha Mosintuwu	357		**KIAT Architects and Thomas Elliott**	
	Eko Prawoto		045	The Hermitage Hotel	126
070	Cemeti Art House	191			
072	Nasirun Gallery	194		**L**	
069	Via Via Café Yogyakarta	190		**L. Martin Sarkies**	
			090	Hotel Majapahit	231
	F			**LABO**	
	F. Silaban		061	Rumah#1	175
033	Bank Indonesia Thamrin	112		**Liauw Goan Sing**	
012	Gelora Bung Karno Main Stadium	74	043	Metropole Cinema	124
032	Istiqlal Mosque	109			
				M	
	G			**Marco Kusumawijaya**	
	Gunawan Tjahjono and Team		018	Komunitas Salihara	84
049	Administration Centre of the University of Indonesia	133	021	Galeri Salihara	89
			074	Bumi Pemuda Rahayu	197
	Ir. Gmeilig Meyling				
057	Concordia	169		**O**	
				Oky Kusprianto	
	H		063	Gupondoro	181
	H. O. K Architect				
014	Bakrie Tower	76		**P**	
	Han Awal			**P. A. J. Moojen**	
080	Bank Indonesia Solo (Extension)	213	044	Tugu Kunstkring Paleis	125
029	Gedung Arsip Nasional (Restoration)	103		**Paul Andreu**	
027	Museum of Bank Indonesia (Restoration)	98	001	Soekarno Hatta Airport	52
				Paul Rudolph	
	Han Awal & Partners		086	Intiland Tower Surabaya	222
079	Bank Indonesia Solo (Conservation)	210	041	Wisma Dharmala	123
008	Gedung Yohanes, Church of St. John the Evangelist	66		**Popo Danes Architect**	
042	Kampus Semangi Universitas Atma Jaya Jakarta	124	107	Popo Danes Studio	294
			115	Ubud Hanging Gardens	313
	Hermawan Dasmanto		117	Villa Bayad	318
088	1903 Restaurant	227			
089	Historica Coffee and Pastry	229		**R**	
	Hidayat Endramukti			**RAW**	
087	De Soematra	224	120	Arumdalu Eco Resort	346
				Realrich Sjarief	
	I		024	Omah Architecture Library	96
	Indra Tata Adilaras				
052	Bogor Raya School	139		**S**	
				SCDA Architects	
	J		108	Alila Villas Soori	297
	J.J.J. de Bruyn			**C. P. W. Schoemaker**	
028	Museum of Bank Mandiri	100	090	Hotel Majapahit	231
				SHL Asia	
	K		102	Villa Alopa	286
	Kerry Hill				
114	Alila Ubud	311			

Society of Ngibikan Village
073 Ngibikan Village
 (Reconstruction) 196
Society of North Nias
(supervised by Yori Antar/Rumah Asuh Foundation)
130 North Nias House
 (Reconstruction) 371
Society of Ratenggaro
(supervised by Yori Antar/Rumah Asuh Foundation)
129 Uma Pangembe of Ratenggaro
 (Reconstruction) 368
Society of South Nias
(supervised by Yori Antar/Rumah Asuh Foundation)
131 South Nias House
 (Reconstruction) 373
Society of Sumpur
(supervised by Yori Antar & Eko Alvarez Z.)
132 Rumah Gadang of Nagari Sumpu
 (Reconstruction) 375
Society of Wae Rebo
(supervised by Rumah Asuh Foundation/Han Awal & Partners)
133 Wae Rebo (Reconstruction) 377
Society of Wainyapu
(supervised by Yori Antar/Rumah Asuh Foundation)
128 Uma Pangembe of Wainyapu
 (Reconstruction) 366
Soejoedi Wirjoatmodjo
009 ASEAN Secretariat 68
031 DPR/MPR Parliament Building 108
Soekarno and Soedarsono
034 Monumen Nasional 112
Sonny Sutanto Architects
103 Oasis Lagoon Sanur 288
Studio TonTon
097 The Bale 275
095 Conrad Wedding Chapel 269
101 Ize Hotel 282
035 Kosenda Hotel 114
023 West One Marketing Office 92
Studiodasar
020 Anjung Salihara 86

T
Tan Tjiang Ay
054 Breeze Art and Boutique Hotel 163
057 Concordia (Additional Functions) 169
017 Kemang 89 83
tim tiga
071 Greenhost Boutique Hotel 192
077 Rempah Rumah Karya 207
078 Rumah Turi 209
Timmy Setiawan
122 Surau Baitul Djalil 350
TYIN Tegnestue Architects
121 Cassia Co-op Training Centre 348

U
UK architect
011 Sequis Centre 73
Unknown Architect
025 Café Batavia 97
Urbane Indonesia
065 Al Irsyad Mosque 184
014 Bakrie Tower 76
123 Mahligai Minang Mosque 351
124 Tsunami Commemoration Museum 354

W
Wastu Adi Olahrupa
096 Amarterra Villas 270
Wija Wawo-Runtu
106 Tandjung Sari Hotel 293
Wiratman & Associates
010 Graha Niaga 71
036 Wisma Nusantara 116
WOHA
099 Alila Villas Uluwatu 279

Y
Y. B. Mangunwijaya
082 Santa Maria Assumpta Church 216
075 Sendangsono Pilgrimage Complex 200
Yori Antar
083 Open Museum of Trowulan
 Archaeological Site 218
051 Plaza Quantum Elektro FTUI 200
Yuli Kusworo
074 Bumi Pemuda Rahayu 197

Z
Zeidler Partnership Architects
039 Wisma BNI 120

Authors

Imelda Akmal

A graduate from the Architecture Department of Trisakti University in Jakarta, Imelda chose to follow a career as a writer specialising in architecture and interior design. In 1992, she began working full-time for various magazines in Indonesia, writing articles on both subjects. Since 1996, she has also published several books related to contemporary Indonesian architecture. Aside from writing, Imelda has produced numerous television programmes in Indonesia. Owing to her publications, she is often asked to speak at public seminars. After she completed her degree in the Master of Business Management at Swinburne University in Melbourne, Australia, and took courses in interior design at the Royal Melbourne Institute of Technology, she established her own writing studio which is called Imelda Akmal Architectural Writer Studio (IAAW Studio).

Imelda Akmal Architectural Writer Studio

Imelda Akmal Architectural Writer Studio (IAAW Studio) is the only Indonesia writing studio to specialise in architecture and interior design. The studio was founded by Imelda Akmal in the year 2002. The studio conducts each stage of the book's composition, from the concept development, writing, styling, photography, layout design, to the printing process in collaboration with the publishers. For over a decade now, IAAW Studio has produced more than one hundred architectural and interior books, many of which have been identified as bestsellers. As of 2010, IAAW Studio has produced bilingual books in Bahasa Indonesia and English-language books for the Asian market. One of IAAW's main commitments is to introduce Indonesian architecture and interior design throughout the world. Imelda is also an active contributor to local and overseas publications.

Photo Credits

Aboday Design: 128; **akanoma:** 359; **Courtesy of Alila Ubud:** 310–311; **Courtesy of Alila Villas Soori:** 296t, 296–297; **Courtesy of Amanjiwo Hotel:** 150–151, 188; **Bambang Tri Atmodjo:** 200, 201; **Billy Gerrardus Santo:** 25, 30–31, 34, 40–41, 51, 52–53, 54, 68–69, 73, 75t, 109, 110–111, 111b, 112, 118, 119, 120, 124, 125, 218–219; **d-associates:** 189; **Duta Cermat Mandiri:** 76t, 121, 164, 166b, 221b; **Dita Kusumawardhani:** 172; **Effan Adhiwira:** 306, 307, 356, 357, 358; **Eko Prawoto:** 194, 195; **Erwinthon P. Napitupulu:** 216, 217; **Fernando Gomulya:** 184; **Courtesy of Green School:** 298–399, 299b, 300, 301; **Han Awal & Partners:** 66t, 103, 138; **Courtesy of Hermitage Hotel:** 126–127, 127t; **Imelda Akmal:** 12, 14, 15, 19, 21, 26, 27, 32–33, 35, 38, 39, 42–43, 44, 45, 46, 47, 48–49, 50, 122, 144–145, 146–147, 148–149, 152–153, 154–157, 158, 159, 160–161, 165, 166t, 167, 168t, 169t, 168–169, 170t, 171t, 170–171, 244–245, 246–247, 248–249, 250–251, 252–253, 254–255, 256–257, 258, 259, 260, 261, 262, 263, 264, 265, 266, 267, 326, 328–329, 330–331, 332, 333, 335, 336–337, 338–339, 340–341, 342–343; **Krishna Aditya:** 286–287, 287; **Oky Kursprianto:** 182, 183; **Pasi Aalto:** 348–349: **Realrich Sjarief:** 96, 346t, 347t, 346–347; **Ridwan Kamil:** 185; **Courtesy of Komunitas Salihara:** 84, 89, 90–91, 91b; **Sie Jie Wan:** 74t, 74–75, 108, 113; **Sjahrial Iqbal:** 180, 181;

Sonny Sandjaya: 16–17, 18, 20, 55, 56, 57, 58, 59, 60, 61, 60–61, 62, 63, 64, 65t, 66b, 67, 70, 71, 72, 76b, 77, 78, 79, 80, 81, 82, 83, 86, 87t, 88, 92t, 92–93, 95–96, 97, 98, 99, 100t, 101t, 100–101, 102, 104, 105t, 106–107, 114, 115, 116–117, 117t, 123t, 129, 130, 131, 132, 133, 134–135, 135b, 136–137, 139, 140, 141, 142, 163, 173, 174–175, 174b, 176–177, 178t, 179, 186, 187, 190, 191, 192, 196, 197, 198–199, 202, 203b, 204–205, 206, 207, 208, 209, 210–211, 212–213, 212b, 214t, 214–215, 220, 221t, 222, 223, 224, 225, 226, 227, 228–229, 229b, 230, 231, 232–233, 233b, 234, 235, 237b, 238–239, 238b, 240–241, 268, 269, 270, 271, 272–273b, 274, 275, 280–281, 282b, 283, 284–285, 288, 289, 290, 291, 292t, 292–293, 294–295, 295t, 302, 303t, 304, 305, 308, 309, 312, 313b, 314–315, 316t, 317t, 316–317, 319t, 318–319, 320, 321, 322–323, 344, 345, 355, 362, 364–365, 366–367, 368–369, 370, 371, 372, 373, 374, 375, 376, 377b, 378–379; **Courtesy of Tandjung Sari Hotel:** 293t; **PT Urbane Indonesia:** 351t, **Courtesy of Villa Uluwatu:** 278–279, 278b; **Witjak Widhi Cahya:** 85, 89, 90–91, 91b.

All other illustrations were taken from the publishers' archive or were made available by the authors or architects.

The *Deutsche Nationalbibliothek* list this publication in the *Deutschen Nationalbibliografie;* detailed bibliographic data are available in the Internet at http://dnb.d-nb.de.

ISBN 978-3-86922-425-1

DOM publishers

© 2015 by DOM publishers, Berlin
www.dom-publishers.com

This work is subject to copyright. All rights are reserved, whether the whole part of material is concerned, specifically the rights of translation, reprinting, recitation, broadcasting, reproduction on microfilms or in other ways, and storage or processing in databases. Sources and owners of rights are stated to the best of our knowledge; please signal any we might have omitted.

Research and Text
Dini Kusumawardhani, Dita Kusumawardhani,
Billy Gerrardus Santo, Alicchys Siregar, Sandra Forestyana

Translation
Jessy Faiz

Proofreading
Clarice Knowles

Maps
Dita Kusumawardhani, Billy Gerrardus Santo, Cintya Pradipta

Layout
Menuk Hidayat

Photo Digital Imaging
Mohamad Aluwi

Final Artwork
Masako Tomokiyo

QR-Codes
Christoph Gößmann

Printing
Tiger Printing (Hong Kong) Co., Ltd.
www.tigerprinting.hk